Tim S. Grover is the CEO ... he founded in 1989, and au... *Relentless: From Good t*... renowned for his work w... Dwyane Wade and thousands of athletes and business professionals, he appears around the world as a keynote speaker and consultant to business leaders, athletes and elite achievers in every field. He is based in Chicago.

Shari Lesser Wenk is the co-writer of Tim Grover's *Relentless* as well as *Start Something* with Earl Woods and the Tiger Woods Foundation. She has been a sports agent and bestselling collaborator since 1983. She lives in Chicago.

Praise for *Winning*

'Tim Grover was by my side for fifteen years, and knows more than anyone about building winners. This book is essential for those who want to be the best at whatever they do ... and are willing to pay the price to get there.' **Michael Jordan**

'Tim Grover is the master of mental toughness. This book is the blueprint for discovering what you are capable of achieving, getting results you never imagined, reaching the highest level of success – and then going even higher.' **Kobe Bryant**

'Tim will take you to the next level, and show you how to be the best at whatever you do. I have unbelievable trust and faith in him.' **Dwyane Wade**

'If you compete at anything – sports or business or life – you need this book. No one knows more than Tim Grover about competitive intensity, killer instinct and crushing the other guy. He is the best at what he does: creating champions.' **Charles Barkley**

'Personal trainer Grover dazzles with his tough-love take on reaching greatness, bluntly advising there are no shortcuts to success ... Those looking for a take-no-prisoners approach to self-improvement will find Grover's philosophy inspiring.' *Publishers Weekly*

ALSO BY TIM S. GROVER

Relentless: From Good to Great to Unstoppable

Jump Attack: The Formula for Explosive Athletic Performance,

Jumping Higher, and Training Like the Pros

W1NNING

THE UNFORGIVING RACE TO GREATNESS

TIM S. GROVER

WITH SHARI LESSER WENK

SIMON &
SCHUSTER

London · New York · Sydney · Toronto · New Delhi

First published in the United States by Scribner, an imprint of
Simon & Schuster, Inc., 2021
First published in Great Britain by Simon & Schuster UK Ltd, 2021
This edition published in Great Britain by Simon & Schuster UK Ltd, 2022

The right of Tim S. Grover to be identified as the author
of this work has been asserted in accordance with
the Copyright, Designs and Patents Act, 1988.

3 5 7 9 10 8 6 4

Simon & Schuster UK Ltd
1st Floor
222 Gray's Inn Road
London WC1X 8HB

www.simonandschuster.co.uk
www.simonandschuster.com.au
www.simonandschuster.co.in

Simon & Schuster Australia, Sydney
Simon & Schuster India, New Delhi

The author and publishers have made all reasonable efforts to
contact copyright-holders for permission, and apologise
for any omissions or errors in the form of credits given.
Corrections may be made to future printings.

A CIP catalogue record for this book
is available from the British Library

Paperback ISBN: 978-1-3985-0194-2
eBook ISBN: 978-1-3985-0192-8

Printed in the UK by CPI Group (UK) Ltd, Croydon, CR0 4YY

For Shari Wenk,
my co-writer and collaborator,
who understood

CONTENTS

W1NNING

THE CHASE

One week before my friend and client Kobe Bryant died in a helicopter crash, we spoke on the phone for the last time.

We hadn't talked in a while, and neither of us apologized for not being in touch more often. We'd send an occasional text just to check in. He was busy. I was busy. All good.

We'd have plenty of time to catch up soon.

Since the end of his basketball career in 2016, Kobe actually seemed busier than he'd been as a player. He may not have been in the gym at 4 a.m. putting up shots as he did for the many years we worked together, but he was still working on new endeavors and obsessions during those dark lonely hours that haunt every true competitor. He'd already won an Oscar, launched a series of bestselling children's books, created several television productions, and was traveling to coach his daughter Gianna's basketball team when the chopper crashed and they were both tragically killed, along with seven others. He hadn't slowed down at all; he was still driven to achieve more and more.

"Rest at the end," he would say, "not in the middle."

During the 2009 NBA Finals, a reporter asked him

why he didn't look happy after his Lakers took a two-game lead over the Orlando Magic. Kobe gave him that iconic Mamba glare, and said:

"Job not finished."

Three words that summed up everything about him.

On that last phone call, we talked for a while, and made plans to get together at the upcoming All-Star game in Chicago. That meeting would never happen.

Our conversation ended like this:

"You good?" I asked.

"Yeah, I'm good. Always chasing that win. Never done."

I hear those words over and over.

Always chasing that win.

Never done.

Kobe's life was a series of wins, fueled by his insatiable hunger to succeed. The more you told him it couldn't be done, the more he wanted to do it. He had to know why, when, how much, how long . . . every detail mattered to him. He couldn't just take a bike ride, he had to ride in the desert, at the hottest time of day, just to prove to himself that he could. He never just watched film, he broke it down frame by frame analyzing every movement, every variation. He played with a concussion in an All-Star game (unbeknownst to anyone else) to see how it would feel. He didn't just call his friend and idol Michael Jordan to ask what's up, he called him in the middle of the night, asking questions and looking for ways to become .0001 percent better. Everything he did, in basketball and in life, was about his desire to win. As an athlete, a father, a creator, a dreamer of what could be next, he looked Winning in the eye over and over, and demanded more. More success, more victories, more accolades, more time with his family.

More time to run his race to greatness.

For all the times Winning said yes to Kobe, on January 26, 2020, it finally said: No.

I know that sounds harsh. I just can't look at it any other way.

Winning doesn't apologize, and it doesn't explain. It throws a party in your honor, refuses to give you the place and time, and sticks you with the check. It pours your champagne, and knocks over the glass.

You reach out to shake its hand, and it has no idea who you are.

Winning puts you on the biggest stage. And shuts off all the lights.

In my thirty-plus years of working with the greatest competitors of our time, from Michael Jordan and Kobe and Dwyane Wade and Charles Barkley and countless others, to CEOs and elite achievers in all walks of life, I've seen Winning in all its glorious generosity, and all its excruciating cruelty. One day it wears a halo. The next day it has fangs.

You don't get to decide which it will be.

You can only chase it, and if you're willing to pay the price, you might catch it. Briefly.

• • •

The ability to win is in all of us. For some, it's the first championship. The first million. The new business. The new house. For others, it's finishing a workout, or finishing school. Sending a kid to college. Buying that first car. Going a whole day without smoking. Ending a bad relationship. Asking for a raise. Seeing the last open parking space, and grabbing it before the other guy gets there. Making a U-turn and getting away with it.

Getting up every day and putting your two feet on the floor.

Winning is everywhere. Every minute, you have the potential to recognize an opportunity, push yourself harder, let go of the insecurity and fear, stop listening to what others tell you, and decide to own that moment. And not just that one single moment, but the next one, and the next. And before long, you've owned the hour, and the day, and the month. Again. Again.

That's how you win.

It doesn't happen all at once. For my athletes, it starts with the first workout in the off-season, builds until the last second of the championship game . . . and continues into the first workout of the next off-season. For my business clients (who play a harder schedule than any athlete) it begins with an unpredictable array of opponents with no off-season, no playbook, and no clock to stop the action, with unofficial scorekeepers and referees who are constantly changing the rules. For everyone, there are endless setbacks, challenges, roadblocks, letdowns, and issues that force most people out of the race.

But if you can stay with it, if you can survive the battlefield in your mind, if you can tolerate fear and doubt and loneliness . . . Winning would like a word with you.

Winning is the ultimate gamble on yourself. The difference between dreaming about what could be, and actually living it.

Winning drives you forward. Every time you advance, you can hear the steel bars clank shut behind you; they are real, and they are earned. Now you can't go back, only ahead. You can't unlearn what you've learned. You can't unfeel what you've felt.

Winning never lies, but it always hides the truth. It tells you everything you want is so close, and then laughs as it slams the door in your face. It tells you all your goals and dreams are impossible, and then taunts you to keep going. One more step. One more step. One more step, to an uncertain destination that might not even be there.

Winning is craziness. It doesn't sleep, and doesn't understand why you do.

It refuses to share time or space with others in your life, like a jealous lover who demands all of you and gets it. It's a driving obsession that looks irrational to others and perfect to you.

Winning is unforgiving. If you screw up, if you lay down, if you show weakness, you're done.

It shows you the best of you, and the worst.

Winning keeps its hands in its pockets, so it doesn't accidentally point to someone unworthy.

It holds you up to the sun. And watches you burn.

If you manage to reach the top, Winning will be there to greet you with open arms. Just before it pushes you off the ledge to make room for someone else.

It's your ultimate reality check, a scorching reminder of who you really are and who you're pretending to be, and forcing you to reconcile the difference. Winning is the lover who takes you to paradise all night long, and disappears before morning. It's the dream you can't remember when you wake up.

Winning is unapologetic. You can be replaced. You *will* be replaced.

I know it's common in books like this for the "experts" to give you "steps." *Five Easy Steps! Ten Secret Steps! Twenty Steps I Just Made Up for This Book!*

Seriously?

You can't buy a map to the top. If you could, everyone would be up there.

They're not.

The steps to Winning are infinite, and constantly shifting. One minute you see a step in front of you, the next moment it's quicksand.

Most people don't see that step disappear until it's too late. They get sucked into the quicksand, and give up.

Winning doesn't care if you can walk up the steps—*anyone* can do that. It wants to know what happens when you miss that step, when you can't see or feel what's in front of you. When you have to trust yourself and believe what you feel, not what you see.

Sometimes you take those steps one at a time, sometimes two at a time. Some days you'll feel so good you'll want to sprint, other days you're crawling on your hands and knees, gasping for breath and wishing you'd never started this race. You'll slip and tumble and lose everything you just gained.

And when you finally make some progress . . . more steps to climb. There's a pebble in your shoe, a blister on every toe. Your lungs want to explode. Every day. Every damn day.

Ten steps?

Wouldn't that be nice.

"Ten steps" are a convenient way to simplify and sell success, but hardly effective.

In 2013, I wrote a book called *Relentless: From Good to Great to Unstoppable*, about mental dominance and the character traits of elite achievers, how they think and act and strategize. I call those individuals Cleaners, and if you read the book, you know there are numerous traits that define a Cleaner. But there is one thing all Cleaners have in common: the ability to achieve the end result over and over. They don't just have a great game or a big month; they have iconic careers that set the standard for everyone else. They take their teams from playoffs to Finals to Championships, they take their businesses from the basement to seven figures to eight figures to three commas. They don't need to be told how. They figure it out and execute. Repeatedly.

I was honored and blessed by the magnitude of support for *Relentless*—from athletes and CEOs, parents and entrepreneurs, entertainers and doctors and presidents and, well, every possible kind of competitor, each running his or her race to greatness. The most common message?

"I thought I was the only one. Thank you for telling me I'm not crazy."

You're not crazy. There are a lot of us out there.

But I was also intrigued by this occasional criticism: "This book doesn't tell you what to do!"

That is correct.

Why the hell do you want to be told what to do?

I don't tell my clients "Be relentless!" or "You got this!" They feel it, they know. The greats fall and stumble and gasp for air just like you do. But they keep going. They already know that at some point, the ground beneath them will shift and give way. They're ready for that; they trust there's another step, even when they can't see it. They don't think about the pain and sacrifice; they just see the end result—Winning. They stay on that road, and they keep chasing greatness.

Thinking back over the years, all my clients chased something. A record. A paycheck. A legacy. A ghost.

MJ chased immortality, and caught it. He will live forever.

Kobe will also live forever. He chased immortality too. But before he could catch it, immortality caught him.

What are you chasing?

What's chasing you?

Because if you're comfortable with sacrifice and pressure and criticism and pain, if you can learn to focus on the result instead of always focusing on the difficulty . . .

you can chase Winning, fight for it, and defend your right to catch it.

But I'm not going to tell you what to do. I'm going to show you an intensely honest and raw picture of what it truly takes to navigate the roadblocks and obstacles and challenges that get in the way, slow you down, and threaten your dreams. I'm giving you the action plan to achieve both success and mastery of the relentless mindset. You can't have one without the other. This is how the greats control and survive the journey, and how you can too. And by the end of this book, you won't have to be told. You'll know.

In April 2020, ESPN and Netflix aired *The Last Dance*, the long-awaited documentary on Michael Jordan and the Chicago Bulls' run for their sixth and final championship together. As MJ's trainer for fifteen years, I considered it a privilege to be included among those who were interviewed and participated in the series.

For many, it was a vividly nostalgic trip down memory lane, with videos and photos and interviews with the greats, stories never told, unfinished business to debate and scores to settle.

For others, it was a bittersweet drama about relentless excellence at all costs. Unapologetic. Unrelenting. Unforgiving. Unforgettable.

For those who lived it, *The Last Dance* was about one thing: Winning. Those years became the platform for my career with the greatest athletes of our time, and the foundation of the work I do today with high achievers in sports, business, and all walks of life . . . those who never stop chasing greatness, however elusive it might be. For more than thirty years, I've witnessed Winning at the highest level, and experienced losing at a level you can't comprehend. I've seen winners lose, and losers win. I've tasted both extremes. My chase continues.

So does yours.

Let me take you into the world of elite cutthroat competition, and show you how to navigate a road that can't be found on any GPS. There is no map, no light, no pavement.

It's the road to paradise, and it starts in hell.

You have been chosen. Not by others, but by yourself.

Welcome to Winning.

THE LANGUAGE OF WINNING

If you're the kind of person who needs to get "pumped up" . . .

If you motivate yourself and others by yelling "Let's do this!" and "You got this!" . . .

If you frequently announce on social media that you "crushed it" and "killed it" and "nailed it" . . .

. . . this is going to hurt.

I don't care. I'm just letting you know.

Winning has its own language, and it doesn't speak bullshit.

Everyone is not a "legend" or a "beast," every event or interview is not "epic" and "life-changing." Every athlete who plays well in the first game of the season is not necessarily "going to be a problem" for the league or anyone else. Everyone driving a Ferrari is not "on fire."

Winning requires real talk. Or, even better, no talk at all.

For example: In the language of Winning, there is no talk about motivation. Motivation is entry level, the temporary rush you get from eating too much frosting. It's that incredible riptide of artificial power and passion and ravenous energy . . . right before it wears off and you're suddenly face-planted on the hard cold floor wondering what the hell happened.

Motivation is for those who haven't decided whether to commit to their goals, or how much time, effort, and life they're willing to invest to achieve them. I'm not measuring their level of success—someone can be broke or out of work or overweight or in a bad situation, and extremely motivated to change that. I'm talking about their need to have others push them into action with a swift kick in the ass.

I don't work with clients who need that kick in the ass. If you come to me, I need to know you're already kicking your own ass, and you're ready for more. Likewise, I'm not a "motivational speaker." I don't write motivational books. I don't want to "fire you up"—that's *your* job. My job is to take your greatest achievements and build on them. I want to speak to you in a language that takes your best work and makes it better.

That's the language of Winning.

So if you expected this book to be about the glory of championship rings and medals and trophies and plaques on the wall, if you're here for poetry about how "You got this!" and "Everyone is a winner," you picked the wrong book. There are no backslaps or participation trophies here. There are no rewards for "showing up." I'm not going to tell you what to wear to the parade.

This is about what you'll go through in the race to greatness. It's about the blood on your hands from a tug-of-war with a ghost you can't see, up to your ankles in shit, surrounded by others trying to bury you in it. The unbearable loneliness and exhaustion. The intense fear of what's ahead for you . . . and what isn't.

If that sounds abnormal, then I'm doing my job here. Ask anyone who has actually won something, in sports or business or anywhere you have to compete with others and with yourself, and they'll tell you the same thing:

There's nothing normal about Winning. If you need normal, if you need to fit in, be prepared for a long stay in the middle of the pack.

Winning requires you to be different, and different scares people. So if you're worried about what others will say, the long-term effects, the sacrifices you'll make, the sleep you'll lose, your family being angry . . . I can't help you with that. There's nothing "typical" about the lifestyle and choices you'll have to make. Winning is inside all of us, but for most, that's where it will stay, trapped under a lifetime of fear and worry and doubt.

The race to greatness has no rules to protect you. Nothing says you're not going to lose, you're not going to get hurt, you're not going to do all this work for nothing. There's no guarantee it will be "fair." Most likely it will *not* be fair. You'll lose at the buzzer. You'll lose to someone who didn't work as hard as you did. You'll lose on a bad call, or a bad play. Someone else will get the job. A pandemic will wipe out your season, your bank account, your career.

Yet the prize at the end of that race remains so compelling, so addictive, so gorgeous, we keep running and stumbling and sacrificing and competing to catch it.

Winning will do everything possible to keep you from catching it, but if you do, if you earn a seat at that magnificent table and you're finally included in the conversation, be prepared for two things: (1) Winning will give you the chair with one broken leg so you can never get comfortable, and (2) you'd better be able to speak its language.

The way you talk about Winning has everything to do with whether you'll achieve it . . . and keep it.

You want to take the vocabulary test I give my clients? It's short and simple:

Describe Winning in one word.

That's it. What does Winning feel like to you? What does it represent?

One word. Take a minute and jot down your first response. You can be honest, this is between you and you. I'm not giving out prizes here.

I've asked this of countless athletes and business professionals and other individuals I work with, and the responses are always revealing. Here are some of the most common answers:

Glorious. Euphoric. Success. Domination. Achievement. Power. Satisfaction. Triumph. Awesome. Amazing.

Not bad answers. If your answer was on that list, you fit right in with the majority. If that's where you want to be.

Of course, *anyone* can fit in. Excellence stands out.

Let me share with you some of the answers I've heard from the greats. Not just in sports but from the business world as well:

Uncivilized. Hard. Nasty. Unpolished. Dirty. Rough. Unforgiving. Unapologetic. Uninhibited.

Kobe: "*Everything.*"

Some people will stare into space, thinking about the enormity of the question. Some get emotional. Some just shake their heads. How do you define the one thing that has consumed and defined your entire life?

I never asked MJ. But he answered it anyway, in *The Last Dance*. In this one moment, he summed up everything he'd learned, everything he'd worked for... everything he knew about his lifelong partnership with Winning. His answer is more than a word, but worth every one:

I pulled people along when they didn't want to be pulled. I challenged people when they didn't want to be challenged, and I earned that right because my teammates who came after me didn't endure all the things that I endured. Once you joined the team, you lived at a certain standard that I played the game, and I wasn't gonna take anything less.

Now if that meant I had to go in there and get in your ass a little bit, then I did that. You ask all my teammates, "The one thing about Michael Jordan was he never asked me to do something that he didn't fucking do."

When people see this, they're gonna say, "Well, he wasn't really a nice guy, he may have been a tyrant." Well, that's you. Because you never won anything. I wanted to win, but I wanted them to win and be a part of that as well.

Look, I don't have to do this. I'm only doing it because it is who I am. That's how I played the game. That was my mentality. If you don't wanna play that way, don't play that way.

And then, famously, "*Break.*"

That unapologetic moment was so raw for him, he had to walk away from the interview momentarily to control the emotion. And that was just within the first hour of filming.

Yes, Winning is glorious and amazing and powerful and awesome and all those things, no one can deny that.

But if you think that's *all* it is, then, as MJ said, you've never won anything.

It's the punishment he took from other teams before elevating himself to becoming the greatest to ever play the game. The years of relentless pressure and scrutiny of everything he did. The single-minded focus on one thing: Winning championships, not just for himself but for everyone around him.

It's Kobe tearing his Achilles but refusing to go to the locker room until he shot—and made—two free throws. The infamous 4:00 a.m. trips to the gym to put up shots, until he could master the shot he missed the night before. The countless hours alone in the dark replaying every game and practice in his mind.

It's Dwyane Wade fighting his way back from surgeries on his knee and shoulder that could have ended the careers of most players, to win two more NBA championships to go with the one he already had, as well as an Olympic gold medal with the 2008 US Men's Basketball team, which he led in scoring. It's Larry Bird playing through debilitating back pain. All the greats of the Jordan era—Charles Barkley, Patrick Ewing, Dominique Wilkins, John Stockton, Karl Malone, Clyde Drexler—realizing they could never win as long as MJ was in the race.

That unforgiving race. Winning can be glorious, but it can also fuck you up.

Think about the greatest achievers you know, the winners, the Cleaners. Think about yourself. What have you gone through to get where you are? What's still ahead of you, seen and unseen? Does it all look like glory and triumph?

If it does, your race is done. I congratulate you.

Now please step out of the way, because the rest of us still have work to do.

Look at these definitions of Winning again:

Uncivilized. Hard. Nasty. Unpolished. Dirty. Rough. Unforgiving. Unapologetic. Uninhibited. Everything.

If that describes your journey and how you attack your goals, we are speaking the same language.

This book is about grit, not glamour. If your image matters more to you than your results, if you need to look and act a certain way to impress others, if "Fake it till you make it" is your strategy for success, if you need approval to be who you really are, you're going to struggle.

If we're working together, I don't need you to be civilized and polite. I need you to be hard. Resilient. Focused. Truthful. I want you completely isolated in your mind, trusting your own voice and instincts to protect you from yourself and others. I want to see you flex the most important muscle in your race to greatness, the one no one sees but you: the I Don't Give A Fuck muscle. We'll be working on that a lot in these pages.

I need you to have a coat of Teflon, so nothing sticks to you and nothing gets in. The more you allow others to get under your skin, so every comment feels like criticism and every criticism makes you lash out, the more that protective coating will wear away, until the hard outer shell becomes soft and weak.

It goes without saying, Winning has zero tolerance for soft and weak.

The greats know how to put on a different face in certain situations that require it, and take it off when it matters. MJ was polite and polished and said the right thing with his sponsors and audiences and interviewers. But put him in his own environment, in the gym, on the court . . . the real guy came out. No inhibitions, no limitations on what he would say or do to get his message across.

Winning ignites a self-conscious awareness that others are watching. It's a lot easier to move under the radar when no one knows you and no one is paying attention. You can mess up and be rough and get dirty because no one even knows you're there. But as soon as you start to win, and others start to notice, you're suddenly aware that you're being observed. You're being judged. You worry that others will discover your flaws and weaknesses, and you start hiding your true personality, so you can be a good role model and good citizen and a leader that others can respect. There is nothing wrong with that. But if you do it at the expense of being who you really are, making decisions that please others instead of pleasing yourself, you're not going to be in that position very long.

When you start apologizing for who you are, you stop growing and you stop winning. Permanently.

The more you win, the more others will try to inhibit your growth, tell you to slow down, stay in your lane. They'll try to keep you in that one lane to control you.

But Winning is about choosing any lane, changing lanes when you need to, and navigating each with equal skill, with an extra gear no one anticipated.

Winners speak a language that doesn't make sense to those who haven't experienced it. A quick glance, a steely stare, a roll of the eyes. Sometimes total silence. You can't explain it, you can't teach it. But when you know, you know. It's not something you broadcast or brag about—"Hey! I'm uncivilized! And also uninhibited!"—because if you have to tell people, it's probably not true. But it's deep inside everyone, if you're willing to just let go and experience your own uncivilized, unapologetic, uninhibited power.

For me, Winning is about all those words and many more, as you will see. It's dead calm, in the midst of total chaos. It can be the greatest joy, and the loneliest feeling in the world. Not everyone feels it this way, you don't have to. I think real winners understand the experience. It's not the whooping and hollering and celebrating, it's that stunning recognition of what just happened. You chased this magnificent thing, this elusive end result . . . and you caught it. You fucking caught it. It's MJ sobbing on the floor, Kobe hugging the trophy alone in the corner. It's the CEO of a billion-dollar empire wondering what happened to the kitchen table that served as his first desk. No one knows what you went through to get there. No one understands what you'll have to do to get there again.

I'm telling you this because when I sat down to write this book, I took my own test and started writing down my own definitions of Winning.

I thought about the wins and losses in every part of my

life: as a child coming to this country with my parents, and witnessing the sacrifice and determination they invested in our family; as a kid dreaming of playing in the NBA, losing my dream to an injury, and admitting to myself that I wasn't good enough; as a young man with a vision of helping professional athletes and having the greatest competitor in history become my first pro client; as a trainer and coach to some of history's greatest champions; as CEO of the world's most respected sports-performance business; as an author and speaker and, above all else, a father.

Winning has been my mentor and my executioner, my greatest ally and most formidable enemy. It's a puzzle of infinite pieces that don't easily fit together, some suspiciously missing—with no picture to show what the puzzle will look like if you ever finish. It's a black hole of desire and greed and insatiable hunger, a careless lover who draws you in and then tells you they're back on the market.

I've looked Winning in the eye long enough to see it wink and turn its back. I've been foolish enough to say, "See you next year," only to hear it whisper: "We'll see."

I've seen what it can do for people, and to people.

What has it done for you? What has it done to you?

Michael rarely speaks about it, and Kobe can't. But they spoke to *me*, in discussions and debates no one else heard or saw, confiding things you haven't read in interviews or children's books. I still study both of them, and often continue those conversations in my mind.

I asked you for your definition of Winning. Now I'm giving you mine.

There are 13. If you read *Relentless*, you may recall that

I like to use the number 13, because I don't believe in luck. Neither does Winning. Winning believes in Winning.

You may also recall that everything on my lists is ranked #1, because when you start ranking things, 1-2-3-4-etc., people think #1 is most important, #2 is less important, and everything else is just there to fill out the list. So we go with #1 for everything, and you can read them in any order.

<u>THE WINNING 13</u>

#1. WINNING makes you different, and different scares people.

#1. WINNING wages war on the battlefield in your mind.

#1. WINNING is the ultimate gamble on yourself.

#1. WINNING isn't heartless, but you'll use your heart less.

#1. WINNING belongs to them, and it's your job to take it.

#1. WINNING wants all of you; there is no balance.

#1. WINNING is selfish.

#1. WINNING takes you through hell. And if you quit, that's where you'll stay.

#1. WINNING is a test with no correct answers.

#1. WINNING knows all your secrets.

#1. WINNING never lies.

#1. WINNING is not a marathon, it's a sprint with no finish line.

#1. WINNING is everything.

This is what I know.

Winning will cost you everything, and reward you with more, if you're willing to do the work. Don't bother to roll up your sleeves, just rip the fucking things off—and do what others won't or can't. They don't matter anyway; you are in this alone.

Stop being afraid of what you'll become. You should be more afraid of *not* becoming that.

If you can't buy into this, if you believe you're not ready or not deserving, if you're not willing to commit to your own success, you've never won, and you probably won't. Because winners all understand one thing: There's a price to pay, and you must pay it.

#1.

WINNING MAKES YOU DIFFERENT, AND DIFFERENT SCARES PEOPLE

When I was training Michael, we set up a schedule that had him training on game days. This was unheard of at the time, and I heard about that from everyone. *Work out on game days? You'll screw up his shot! He'll be fatigued! He'll be less athletic!*

Working out makes you less athletic?

We saw it differently.

Think about it. He played three to four games a week, plus travel days, plus practice, plus rest days. When was he supposed to train?

No one really had an answer for that, because daily workouts were not the norm in the NBA at that time, nor were they a high priority. Very few players were on a regular training regimen, especially during the season, and none brought in someone from outside the organization to train them. MJ was the first, when he hired me.

Remember, he brought me in specifically to add muscle and power to his body, because he knew it would help him get past the bigger, stronger players who were physically beating him on the court. As his game elevated, so did the physical intensity he faced from every opponent, and he realized that to get to next level and win, he had to do something different. The Bulls had a conditioning program for their players, but he wanted—and needed—more.

He was my first professional athlete: The world's greatest basketball player was working with a trainer who had never trained a pro. Improbable? Yes. Crazy? Maybe. But crazy—combined with the willingness to take a chance—is the secret weapon of Winning, and we both had an impressive arsenal of crazy.

If you think like everyone else, if you act like everyone else, if you follow the same protocols and traditions and habits like everyone else, guess what: You'll *be* like everyone else.

Everyone wanted to be like Mike.

Mike did not want to be like anyone else.

Which led us to training on game days.

If our goal was to continuously add muscle and make him stronger—as well as minimize injuries and preserve his longevity—it would have been counterproductive to ignore his training every time he had a game. Believe me, I studied and researched and tested him and looked at every possible variable that could impact his performance. We kept every game day consistent—trained the same muscles, did the same kind of workout, accounted for every component that might affect his shot and his endurance, eliminated as many of those variables as we could, so his body became prepared to play under the same conditions, regardless of the game schedule. It became such a part of his routine that when we didn't work out, he'd feel the difference and comment, "Something doesn't feel right."

Bottom line, it worked for him, and obviously the results spoke so clearly that I never had to respond to everyone who said it wouldn't work at all.

It was never about being different for the sake of being different, or generating publicity, or trying to look clever and progressive.

It was about understanding the difference between knowing how to think, and being told what to think.

Winners engage their minds and experiences to create new levels of greatness. I'm not just talking about athletes here, I'm talking about innovators and groundbreakers in business, entertainment, science, technology, education, medicine, parenting . . . every walk of life. Bill Gates personally checking every line of code for the first five years of Microsoft's existence. Jeff Bezos shipping books out of his garage. Sara Blakely cutting the feet off her pantyhose. Elon Musk gazing up at Mars. They weren't afraid to think originally, they weren't worried about what others would think about their "crazy" ideas. That whole BS about thinking outside the box is just that: BS. Winners don't see the box. They see possibilities. They use their own decisions, successes, and failures as a springboard to elevate their thinking and results.

Every great creation and invention started with people who knew how to think and didn't allow themselves to be told what to think. If you want to get to the elite level, this is what sets you apart. If you follow the textbook exactly, if you always do it the "normal" way, you can be very good at what you do. But what happens when there's a glitch or an unforeseeable issue that the textbook didn't cover? How do you manage when nothing is "normal"? People love to talk about "pivoting" in hard times—making a fast shift in a different direction—but you have to pivot and move *toward* something, you can't keep changing direction just to change direction. And unless you know how to think for yourself, you're just going to keep pivoting back and forth, this way and that way, waiting for someone to save you. Waiting to be told what to think.

If I gave you a piece of paper with a thousand dots, and told you to connect them, how would you attack that challenge? Would you form a picture of something recognizable? Would you create random shapes and designs? Would it look like a crazy doodle? Would you just tear it up?

Those dots are your map of the race to greatness. You can go in a straight line, you can chart your own course, you can wander aimlessly. You can ask others how to get where you're going. You can quit.

For me, those dots are about watching how a winner moves, and figuring out how I can make him move better. I know how everyone else sees him, can I see him differently? Can I take him in another direction? Can I make him fly? That's the artwork I see in those dots, the result of everything I've learned from others and elevated with my own knowledge. I know there's already a picture out there telling me what to do. I don't want that. I want to create my own.

Winning watches to see if you're confident and bold

enough to believe that "different" isn't wrong. It's the difference between lighting your own fire and waiting for someone to light it for you. To me, curiosity is the spark that lights that fire. I have a habit of staring at people, not to be rude, but to study and learn about them. I know it can make others uncomfortable, which is not my intention, but I believe it makes me good at what I do; I'd rather observe someone closely than rely on what I'm told.

Are you asking questions? Do you allow your mind to wander into new possibilities and scenarios, no matter how far-fetched and unattainable they might seem, like you did when you were a kid? Kids understand curiosity. They see something interesting and they have to play with it, eat it, throw it . . . they can't leave it alone. For a few minutes, it's the greatest thing they've ever known, until an adult comes along and takes it away. They'll ask question after question after question . . . until the adult can't take it anymore and tells them to stop asking so many questions.

That was MJ and me in the beginning of our relationship. There was so much I wanted to know, so much I knew I could learn from him. I'd ask about everything, until he finally said, "Man, you ask so many questions." I kept on asking. I already knew what I was *supposed* to think about him, and I knew what everyone else thought about him. I needed to know more than that.

Kobe did the same thing with him; he'd call or text Michael in the middle of the night asking how he played against a certain guy, how he handled a situation, what he thought about this or that. And Michael would always answer his questions, and help him learn. That's a major trait of the greats, by the way: They want to pass along their knowledge, so the next generation can keep learning.

That's the difference between competing and winning.

I hear this all the time from my corporate clients: "We know how to compete. Now we need to learn how to win." It's not always the same thing.

When you know what to think, you're ready to compete. When you know *how* to think, you're ready to win.

Your education teaches you what to think. Life experience teaches you how to think. In school, you're tested after you learn. In life, the test comes before you learn.

Coaches and bosses tell you what to think. Doing the work tells you how to think.

Your parents show you what to think. Adulthood shows you how to think . . . if you're open to learning.

If you follow a recipe for the perfect chocolate cake, you'll get that exact cake because you were told what to do. But after you've made it a few times, maybe you start thinking of a way to make it even more perfect, so you change something in the recipe. And you were right; it turned out even better. That's about *how* to think, not *what* to think.

You can go into a big chain restaurant, order the mac and cheese, and have complete confidence that you'll find the exact same meal in a hundred other locations, prepared exactly the same way. There's a system in place, with procedures and guidelines, and if you're in charge of preparing that dish, you don't have the option to think of a better way to make it.

Master chefs have countless ways to make that dish,

never the same way twice. *How* to think, not *what* to think.

Thinking for yourself creates independence, which many of the self-help "experts" out there dread, despite their promises to the contrary. Why? The more you think for yourself, the less you'll need the "experts." If you're always reading self-help books and listening to motivational talkers and following inspirational geniuses on social media and podcasts, if you can't make a decision without consulting mentors and masterminds . . . you're being told what to think. You're being told, *I'm successful, this is how I did it, this is what I believe, so you should believe it too.* And it all makes sense, sounds so good, so you accept it as truth. But how do you *know*? Are you experiencing it? Using it? Are you staying with it long enough to fully absorb what you're learning, or are you jumping ahead to the next hot thing? Are you putting action behind all that advice, so you can find out for yourself? You may be getting a lot of great guidance and knowledge, but it's always going to be someone else's knowledge, until you question it, adapt it, and find out for yourself if it works for you.

Kobe used to say, "Knowledge is power." And I'd tell him: "Only if you use it." He definitely used it.

And yes, I know this applies to me and my books and the ideas I share with you, and if this topic makes you stop and think about how to adapt what I told you and apply it differently to your own life, then I'm doing my job. I want you to question what I believe. It's precisely the reason some readers griped that *Relentless* didn't tell them what to do.

I'm not going to tell you what to do. I'm not going to tell you what to think. I want you to learn HOW to think, to become involved in the process of learning so you can create your own ideas and thoughts, answer your own questions, and know how to create solutions when others don't even understand the issues.

I work with my sports and business clients the same way when we're working on mental toughness and focus. At first, most want to talk every week, with a standing appointment. But I don't work that way, because to me, that's just waiting to be told what to do, every week at the same time. *Oh good, it's Tuesday, now I can deal with this issue I should have handled five days ago but instead I waited for my scheduled call with Tim.* We'll still talk on a regular basis, but not just because we're "supposed to." I want them thinking for themselves, working on their own abilities to make decisions and manage issues. I want to see them create ways to win, and execute those ideas without running them by me first. That's how you learn to think for yourself.

Sometimes when clients are on a hot streak, I don't want to talk to them at all. My total communication with them might be a look or a nod, and many times, that says it all. They already know and *feel* things are going well; I don't want to alter their thinking. We don't need to discuss what's going right, they just need to keep doing it.

Everyone looks for the "key" to Winning, like you can carry it in your pocket and pop it into a lock. There is no key; it's a combination vault of infinite numbers and infinite outcomes, with rusted, decayed dials that barely move, and digits that have been rubbed bare by countless desperate fingers trying to turn them in their favor.

Most people will solve some of the combination, but they give up trying to figure out the rest and settle for what they have. A select few will keep fiddling with the dials, hoping to get those last couple of numbers.

But if you stay with it long enough, if you can elevate your thinking and your expertise to a level that allows you to figure out the complete combination, you can bust the lock on Winning's heavily guarded fortress.

And while you're celebrating, Winning is already changing the combination.

For me, the challenge has always been about working that combination so I can find new ways to make great competitors even greater. I can't get them there by applying the same techniques everyone else uses, because we're not talking about getting 10 percent better or 5 percent better. The goal is .0001 percent better, because these performers are already among the best at what they do. Consider an athlete like Michael Phelps, for example, who won twenty-three Olympic gold medals (and twenty-eight medals overall) by finding ways to shave a hundredth of a second off his times. You can't achieve that by training and thinking like everyone else, you have to be innovative and dedicated enough to go where others can't or won't. So when I'm working with a competitor who is so elite that he's literally competing against himself, I have to combine all the research and teachings and data, add the unique component of his specific needs and challenges, and create solutions that are unique to him.

When I was training MJ, the Bulls' strength coach asked why I had him doing bicep curls. The theory was that biceps were just for show and didn't really make someone a better basketball player. And that was probably true. But we were going for that .0001 percent, which included the intimidation factor of his bigger, stronger, more dominant physique. What's the first thing you see on a basketball player when he takes off his warm-ups? Those arms.

Details matter.

It works the same in business. Look at a company where everyone has the same training, the same procedures, the same rules and regulations, the same products and services to sell. Everyone represents the same name on the logo. But some will excel, above and beyond, because they advanced their skills and their thinking. That's the difference between learning what is handed to you, and understanding how to build on that.

Winning requires you to learn, question what you learned, and then learn more. You have to be willing to challenge what you've been taught, and learn it again with a different perspective. Everything I've done with my clients has been the result of helping them close the gap between being the best, and being the best *ever*. Big difference between those two. I had to challenge traditional training techniques, and learn them all over again through the lens of what I was discovering on my own. None of my college professors ever advised me to take the greatest athlete who ever played, have him train on game days, and give him a steak a few hours before tip-off.

Yes. He ate steak before games.

Back in the eighties and nineties, the nutrition prescription for athletes was carbs, carbs, and more carbs. Everyone was eating rice and pasta for fuel, but that wasn't working for MJ: Aside from feeling bloated, he was playing so hard that it just wasn't enough for him. When the team was playing at home, he was eating at 3:30 in order to get to the stadium by 6:00. So he was starving by the 7:30 game time, and by the fourth quarter, he could feel his energy decreasing.

So we added a small steak to his pregame meal.

Now, listen: I'm not telling *you* to eat steak before a game, I'm not giving you nutritional advice here. I'm telling you we had to devise a new plan for Michael, based on his body chemistry and schedule, his playing minutes, and the massive amount of energy he expended on the court. The steak slowed down the digestion of everything else he was eating—the starches, vegetables, etc.—and kept his blood sugar consistent so he had more energy throughout the entire game. It wasn't something I learned in a book or nutrition class, it just made sense to me. I knew what we'd tried and what hadn't worked. Let's do this instead, we can always try pasta or something else at halftime. But for now, we'll try steak.

Believe me, I've tried a lot of ideas that didn't work at all. I've spent hours putting together the perfect program, only to take my client through the workout and realize within five minutes that I have to throw out the whole thing. I'm not a genius, far from it. I'm not going to tell you I always know the answer. But I'm going to keep trying solutions until I find it.

Winning demands that you look past "the right way"

and create your own way. Coaches love to ridicule players who bend over when they feel fatigued; they say it's a sign of weakness and tell them to stand up straight instead, with hands on their head. It never made sense to me, even when I was playing. You're telling me that if I'm fatigued, I'm supposed to hold my arms over my head to open my lungs more? If I'm breathing hard while training or playing, my lungs are already open. It always felt more natural to me to bend forward.

So I finally told Michael, "Grab your shorts." He thought I was crazy. "Just do this," I said. "Bend over when you need a second to catch your breath, and grab the bottom of your shorts." Not hands on his knees, because I didn't want him putting pressure on his knees. But when he started grabbing the bottom edge of his shorts, he realized he was able to breathe more deeply, and recovered so much faster. You can search the Internet for yourself, and find hundreds of pictures of him on the court, between plays, holding the edge of his shorts.

We worked on every possible detail: fingers, toes, ankles . . . everything that could go wrong, we addressed it. It's no coincidence that he played every game most of our years together; we created the opportunity for that to become a reality. That was our style of "load management": managing his body to play the complete load of eighty-two regular season games, plus potentially twenty-six more in the playoffs as well as the preseason.

How to think, not *what* to think.

With Kobe, there were very few things he wouldn't try in his training, if he believed we could get that .0001 percent. When I first told him about bending over to catch his breath, he said he wouldn't do it because it didn't look good. Winning makes everyone look good, I told him. He tried it. It worked.

We took bike rides in the Vegas desert at high noon so he could train in the most challenging conditions. We flew to Europe to try the first cryotherapy chambers, where we literally walked around inside a frigid chamber, totally immersed in temperatures that make today's cryo tubes feel toasty. I had him eat pizza as a pregame meal when he had back-to-back games, because it boosted his energy and stamina. Even his decision to use a helicopter on game days, from Orange County to Staples Center, was about thinking of new ways to get that slight edge, because it gave him time away from everything and everyone before a game. I know the helicopter came to represent catastrophic tragedy, but he had no fear of what could go wrong. If he thought something would give him an advantage, he wanted it.

It's no coincidence that the greats figure out what works for them, regardless of what everyone else does. Dwyane didn't just work out on game days, he liked to work out right before the game. He preferred to be at home in the mornings; that was his time to relax. So before home games I'd meet him at the arena at 6:00 p.m., before game time, and we'd go through a set of movements for around twenty minutes, take practice shots for ten minutes away from the crowd, just enough to get his body feeling the way he wanted it to feel. He had the whole weight room and practice court to himself, and he used that time to mentally and physically prepare. No one told him to do that; it was his way of creating an environment and schedule that allowed him to perform at a higher level.

LeBron James is another great who figured out his own path to Winning. He essentially created the "superteam" phenomenon in the NBA, by deciding where he wanted to play and with whom, knowing he'd be criticized for going against the way others had managed their careers in the past. Everyone was telling him what to think, where to play, and what to do. He exercised his right to think for himself, and changed not only the course of his career but the direction of the NBA.

I hear from players every season who say, "Let's work together, I'll do whatever it takes." Then I tell them what it takes, and they can't even comprehend what I'm talking about. Not because it's so complex, but because it's not what they're accustomed to. They've always trained one way; it's all they know. But if you're not getting results doing what you know, if you need to plan our work around your vacations, if you get injured every season and can't figure out why . . . maybe it's time to think about new ways to achieve what you're chasing.

To me, it isn't about what's right or wrong, it's about deciding what you will or won't negotiate for yourself, and whether you're willing to expand your thinking in a way that allows you to move closer to Winning than your competition.

People get caught up in their "nonnegotiables," those rules and beliefs that can't be altered because . . . because . . . why? Because everyone says so? Because that's the way you've always done it? You can tell yourself over and over that you won't negotiate your dreams, your goals, your plans, but if you get to the point where those things aren't working, you might have to start negotiating with yourself. Not with others. With yourself.

You have to be careful with nonnegotiables, because while it sounds tough and badass to announce what you absolutely will and will not do, there are infinite things that can get in the way and force you to change direction. Most people did not begin 2020 planning to homeschool their kids or work from the kitchen table. They didn't plan on their gyms closing. My athletes didn't plan on living in a bubble or playing shortened seasons; my corporate clients didn't plan on running their businesses via Zoom calls. Try clinging to your nonnegotiables when everything you planned is suddenly yanked out of your grasp.

Your nonnegotiables have to be things you—and only you—can control. The food you eat. The effort you commit. The words you speak. The results you deliver.

If you can't personally control the outcome, you're dealing in goals that will potentially require you to adapt, change direction, get creative, and think differently about managing the obstacles that block your path. *Our team is going to win the title. Our business is going to triple its revenue. My kid is going to med school.* Nonnegotiable? Or wishful thinking?

Winning hears your promises, and laughs out loud. If you don't control it, you'd be better be prepared to negotiate for it. And the negotiation never stops.

I've seen great competitors get to the top by refusing to negotiate their ambition to win. They made every right choice, committed the time and effort, and did the work better than anyone. But as soon as they won, they renegotiated everything. The celebration began, the pressure was off, the priorities changed, and the focus on Winning was suddenly blurred by the pursuit of countless *other* things.

For my clients, I have one nonnegotiable: Performance. Everything contributing to that is open to discussion, as long as we arrive at the same end result. If it helps you to train on a game day, if you perform better with a steak in your diet, if you want to ride a bike in the 120-degree desert, you have my full support . . . as long as your performance proves the benefits.

You need to have that drink? Okay with me. I know all the studies on the effects of alcohol on performance, but I have also seen firsthand what a glass of wine can do to relax the body and mind. I'm not prescribing it or telling you to do it. If you need to go to that party and have some fun, I understand, but if your performance starts to make people wonder where you were the night before, now we're going to need some limits and restrictions. Because the one thing we're not going to negotiate is anything that adversely impacts your performance. If you're out until 5:00 a.m., if you had a lot to drink, if you smoke to relax, I'll judge you by your results. Did you play like garbage the next day? We're going to have a talk about what happened the night before. You played *great*? Remind me what you did the night before; we might need to do that again.

I can't remember all the times I trusted my own thinking and succeeded. But I can remember the times I ignored my own thoughts, did what I was told to do, and failed.

A few years ago, I was speaking to a huge audience of business owners, mostly male, very affluent, very conservative. There were several speakers at this event, and I was the closing keynote. The organizer of the event made one request of all the speakers: No cursing. "We don't really mind, but the audience is very conservative," we were told, "and we don't want to offend anyone."

Now, I can curse, or I can not curse. I'm sure it won't surprise you to know I'm much more comfortable when I can be myself on the stage, which means occasionally cursing. But I'm also respectful of groups and audiences who don't enjoy that, and I always comply when asked to keep it clean.

So I'm waiting to take the stage, and I'm listening to the guy who is speaking ahead of me. He's a former Navy Seal, talking about leadership and teamwork . . . and he's using words I wouldn't even whisper in a locker room. Not a single sentence without an f-bomb. And I look out into the audience . . . and they are loving it. Laughing, clapping, with a huge standing ovation at the end.

And now I have a decision to make. I gave these people my word there'd be no cursing, at least from me. Do I break my word and ignore their request, as he did, because I know the audience will enjoy the talk I want to give, or do I follow the rules and keep it clean?

I kept my word, because that's a nonnegotiable for me, and I followed the rules. And it was the first time I hated my own speech.

Not because I used clean language—I was being respectful, which was the appropriate thing to do—but because

I let someone else tell me what was "right," when I knew they were wrong.

And that is also a nonnegotiable for me.

One of my nonnegotiable core values is trusting my instincts, and believing what I know. I might be wrong, but I want the chance to be right. And I'd rather decide for myself than allow others to decide for me.

Winning does not negotiate. You won or you lost. It doesn't care how hard you worked, it doesn't care about extenuating circumstances that got in your way. *You worked hard? That's nice. I need someone who works hard, smart, fast, and a whole mess of other things. Get back in line and figure it out.*

Figure it out. Put your craziness to work. Innovate, don't imitate. And above all, stop listening to everyone who tells you what to think. If they knew, they'd all be winners.

#1.

WINNING WAGES WAR ON THE BATTLEFIELD IN YOUR MIND

I don't know a better way to say this, so if it offends you . . . well, that's on you:

Winning fucks with your mind.

It just does.

There's nothing else that can whip you around faster and harder. You're just getting started, and instantly it's over. You're feeling calm and cool, and suddenly you're burning up. You're face-to-face with triumph, when you feel it slap you from behind. You're completely in charge, until you realize someone else is controlling everything. You finally get your arms around Winning . . . and it leaves you on the floor gasping for breath.

You give everything you have for one glorious victory . . . and discover it isn't ever going to be enough.

Like I said. Winning fucks with your mind.

There's no way you can't be affected by it.

That's true for the greatest champions in history, and equally true for anyone who has ever craved victory and achieved it: One minute they're exploding with joy at the moment of triumph, and a day later they're facing the reality that to keep that feeling, they have to do it all over again. And this time it will be twice as hard.

Winning is a war. And it's fought on the battlefield in your mind.

On this battlefield, there is no rest. Your mind never stops. You have no peace.

I don't care if you're living in a twelve-bedroom mansion or on a friend's couch in the garage. When you're in the race to win, you spend every night sleeping with the enemy. And that enemy is you: the one person who knows all your weaknesses and fears, knows everything you crave and dread, and never stops using them against you.

Winning fills your head with a minefield of ideas and warnings and questions . . . and detonates them all at once. Your thoughts keep fighting even when you're asleep, preparing for the threat of imagined battles that haven't happened yet. They might happen. They might not.

You go to bed tired and wake up tired because there's a raging onslaught of chaos in your head, and there's no nap that can erase that. The minute you wake up, you're fighting again. Your mind is so overrun with conflict that you can't even remember going to sleep.

All day, every day, your mental battlefield is attacked by blasts of adrenaline and anger and fear and anxiety, and other explosives too. Stress. Insecurity. Doubt. Envy. Sometimes it's a stranger who puts them there. Sometimes it's someone close to you. Sometimes it's you. Most of the time, it's you.

If you look closely, you can read the labels on the bombs:

You can't win. Terrible idea. Everyone is laughing. You look ridiculous. This is going to cost too much. Fuck those people.

Not all of those mines are cruelly harsh; they can also be dangerously kind: *You should take the day off. You work too hard. You're better than the others. They have no chance. You've already won. Relax, enjoy. Don't take everything so seriously.*

Winners can detect those bombs and defuse them before they can do any damage. Losers brace for impact and wonder how to clean up the mess.

You know all about those explosives, and you know exactly what's going to set them off. But by the time you're ready to deal with them, you're tired. Distracted. Confused. You're trying to find peace, a calm, serene place to think, and instead you find yourself in a wild mental war zone with smoke and explosions and all kinds of screaming, probably yours. And just as you're about to diffuse this one ticking time bomb, you feel another blast detonating, and it's five times more explosive. One minute you're managing sparklers, and the next thing you know, a grenade just went off over there. You're fighting fires everywhere, and as soon as you extinguish one, another bursts into flames.

Everyone wants to "set the world on fire." But you also have to control how it burns.

Winning loves that battle: *How much can you take? How far can I push you? Are you having fun yet?*

I don't care how much skill and talent you have, what plans you've dreamed, what promises you've made. If you can't dominate this battlefield, you can't win.

This is your space, your territory. It's yours to dominate, or someone else will.

Are you able to extract those explosives from the minefield? Do you have the mental strength and agility? Are you aware of the distractions, insecurities, and false beliefs planted in your mind?

This is what enables great winners to separate from everyone else. They have losses and failures, they face criticism and commentary and all kinds of obstacles. But they consistently possess the stark ability to win those mental battles, shut them down, and move on to the next fight.

Your mental battlefield is the command center of every decision you make. If you decide something is a problem, then it's going to be a problem. When you wake up in the middle of the night worrying about money, you can either figure out a way to handle your finances or you can lay in the dark worrying about how you'll never dig out. Before a big game or important meeting, you can think of all the ways you could screw up, or you can mentally walk through the details you'll need to make it all work. When you make a mistake, when you experience failure, you can step on the mine that explodes the "LOSER!" bomb, or you can navigate yourself to a better place where you have the clarity to plan your next move.

Trust me, I'm not going to talk to you about the BS of "positive thinking" and "visualizing." You can visualize being a winner, you can envision that moment of glory, you can think positive about how it's all going to work. It's a nice daydream, but daydreaming is as effective as calling a disconnected number. Wake up. None of that has happened yet. Winning doesn't visit you in your dreams . . . it sees you in your nightmares.

What are the thoughts that dance into your head in the middle of the night when it's finally quiet enough for you to hear yourself think? *Did I get enough done? Could I have worked harder? Can I do this? Am I kidding myself? Am I ever going to make it?*

Those thoughts can trigger disaster for many who fear they're failing; they wake up every day in a panic, facing another day of anxiety and dread. *I have no idea what I'm doing. I'm a fraud and everyone is going to see it. I'm never going to make it. I'm a mess. I can't do this.*

But for others, those thoughts are a blueprint for improvement. *Did I get this right? Can I do better? I know what to do, I need to make that happen.* And they move in on those bombs, inspecting them from every angle, until they can extract and defuse them.

That was Kobe. *I can't rest until I make this shot I should have made today.* He'd be playing that moment over and over in his head, trying to figure out what happened so it didn't happen again. He'd relive the game in his mind, watching film at 4:00 a.m., until he could understand why he missed that shot. *What was going on with the defense? Where was the ball? Did it rotate correctly? Was it wet? Was it heavy? Was my head too far back? Did I catch it right? Was my elbow correct?* He'd go through every possible variable until he could answer his own questions, and know with some certainty that the answer in his mind would resolve the issue on the court.

Everything you do starts with your thoughts. How many times have you sabotaged your own goals and ambitions because your head wasn't in the right place? You wanted to lose ten pounds, but the pizza looked so good. You wanted to quit drinking, but what the hell, it's been a hard day. You knew you should have made that one phone call, but you weren't sure what to say. You had all your plans in place to make a major move in your life . . . and you let someone talk you out of it.

No one forced you into those choices. You just weren't prepared to win those battles.

I've watched great players lose everything because they couldn't make that mental leap from wanting to win to making it happen. They started believing the hype and the bullshit, and stopped believing in what got them there in the first place.

This is not just about athletes, of course. It can happen to anyone, in any endeavor. I see it all the time with the business leaders and entrepreneurs I work with: One day they're on a clear trajectory toward success, and then suddenly they can't win at all. What happened? They didn't suddenly forget how to execute. Something else got in the way, and it's almost always something mental.

I've dealt with so many athletes with brilliant talent, whose careers were completely destroyed inside their mental bomb shelters. They believed every gratuitous compliment about their greatness, every grandiose tribute to their excellence. From the time they were kids, they were told how special they were, which may have been true enough at the high school or collegiate level. Unfortunately, they hadn't actually accomplished anything at the pro level, and instead of working harder to match their alleged potential, they bought into the hype and focused on "building their brand" instead of their results.

Note: Get the results, and the brand will build itself. Play it the other way around, and your career will be dead long before your shoe deal expires.

That's how you sabotage yourself.

Are you winning your own war? People find so many ways to derail their own success. Distractions, laziness, ego . . . Winning has a million ways to stop you, if you don't have the resilience to fight back.

How well do you deal with distractions? I'm sure you know people—including yourself—who have no ability to filter and manage issues with family and friends, addictions, financial problems, relationships, health, legal trouble . . . everything that happens to them is their new reason for not getting to the finish line. They give their time and energy to everything and everyone, and then blame all those things that "got in the way," without ever once recognizing that the biggest obstacle in the way was themselves. And at the end of the day, their focus is on everything except the one thing that could have made it all work—Winning.

I'm not talking about distractions like watching videos on your phone or texting your friends or wandering into the kitchen for your fifteenth snack of the evening, although those are definitely distractions. I'm talking about the internal distractions caused by your own mental combat with yourself.

If you're procrastinating, if you're constantly apologizing for things you did and didn't do, if you get to the end of the day and realize you didn't accomplish a single thing you wanted—or needed—to do, you're distracted by your own thoughts.

We all have some kind of "To Do" list, but for most, it's a "Things to Do That Will Never Get Done" list.

Winners have a "Done" list.

You have a list that never gets shorter? Things you just can't seem to accomplish, because you never have the time, or knowledge, or money, or approval from others, or whatever you claim is stopping you? Things you could have done when you were quarantined at home during the Covid-19 pandemic, with literally nothing to do even after you watched every possible Netflix series?

Do yourself a favor: Either do them, or admit you're never doing them and move on. Managing that "back burner" is a ridiculous waste of time and energy; all those burners generate the same amount of heat anyway, and those things stay on your mind and taunt you every time you start thinking about everything you've left unfinished—or unstarted. Get rid of them. You'll feel better immediately.

Distractions can be fatal to your goals, if you don't manage them. Notice I said "manage," not "eliminate." I know, you've been told a thousand times to "eliminate distractions." Not possible. You might be able to erase some, but people are still going to need you, there will still be tasks and chores to do, the phone and the TV and the refrigerator are still going to be there, taunting you. And if those things are so distracting, enough that they've created an issue, they'll be even more distracting when you try to eliminate them.

If you want to manage distractions and get control of that battle, you need to put some routines in place.

I'm not talking about sticking with old routines designed to keep you comfortable and safe and get you through the day without "rocking the boat," because sometimes, that boat needs to be rocked. Hard. If you never rock that boat, how will you know how much it can take? This isn't about fighting boredom or dealing with anxiety or avoiding new things. I don't want to see you sleepwalking through your life, just getting by. We all know people who are just plodding through every day. They say things like, *Another day another dollar... Easy come easy go... Sun up sun down... Just glad to be here ... Same old same old*. If that's you—and I seriously hope it's not—you need to blow up that routine, and replace it with something that engages you mentally and helps you create new challenges and results.

To me, routines are freedom, if you use them correctly. They allow you to take action with certainty and purpose; they remove the variables and speed bumps that slow you down. And most important, they bypass the battlefield decisions: *Should I? Should I not? This way? That way? Today? Tomorrow? How long? Who should I ask?* When you have a well-planned routine, those questions have already been answered. You execute and move on. Done. Next.

MJ had the most disciplined game-day routine I've ever seen, from the way he selected his timepiece to the way he laced his shoes. He planned and organized every detail of his day, from the time of his workout to the car he drove to the arena. He put his clothes on in a specific order, organized the game tickets for his family and friends, ate at the same time every day . . . everything had purpose and discipline.

And everyone on his personal team participated in those routines. I knew what time and how long we were working out (5:00 a.m., 6:00 a.m., or 7:00 a.m. every day, even on road trips and travel days). His automobile manager knew which car he'd be driving, and what time to have it washed and ready (MJ would never take a car that hadn't just been washed). The chef knew exactly what he'd be eating, and what time we needed it served. Everything was planned and coordinated, so there were no bumps in the schedule.

Part of his routine was to lace his shoes before every game, fresh out of the box. The ritual had special meaning to him; every time he did it, he could remember that feeling of being a kid getting new shoes, and it took him to a place that prepared him mentally for the game and helped put him in the zone. One day on the road the team bus was delayed coming into the arena, so I went ahead and laced his shoes exactly the way he did, just to save him some time. He refused to wear them: I'd interfered with his routine. He had the equipment manager get him a new pair—unlaced—so he could lace them himself.

He practiced and played in a routine as well. Every

time he warmed up in practice, he started with a chest pass. The greatest player in the world, working on a basic chest pass. Why? Routine. Basics. Fundamentals. The court was his battlefield, and he knew where all the mines were planted. If you can't master the fundamentals, you can't master anything else.

Even before games, in the tunnel, he would go through the motion of a chest pass, watching an imaginary ball release perfectly off his fingers and thumbs, spinning its way through his mind, cutting through the unnecessary thoughts in his head.

His fundamentals were so well rehearsed, he never had to think about those basics during a game. He knew if he could get to a certain spot on the court, nothing could stop him. Most players have a spot like that. MJ had them all over the floor; that was his minefield. He knew exactly where to position himself, and where his doomed opponents would be blown up.

No different from elite military executing a complex operation. Routine isn't an option, it's imperative. Every detail is planned, mapped, and required; the team has to work in complete synchronization, or everyone is at risk. From the way you're taught to make your bed, to the precision and accuracy of jumping out of a plane, there is no room for creative options; the decisions have been made for you. Don't think. Execute.

Part of MJ's greatness was that ability to execute; even the smallest details of his movements enabled him to act and react faster than almost anyone else on the court. He could get his shots off quickly because he caught the ball with his knees bent, and his shoulders already squared up to the shot, so he was already in position to shoot. Most players catch the ball, and then get in position to take the shot. MJ was already there; the gun was already locked and loaded. He rarely had to reposition his body or turn his shoulders after the pass; all he had to do was catch and turn his head to see the basket.

To this day I don't even know if that was something he learned, or if it just came naturally to him. But it eliminated a split second of not having to think about those extra steps, not having to waste physical and mental energy.

That's how you control your mental battlefield.

Why was routine so important to him? Because the games themselves were so unpredictable. Not uncontrollable, but unpredictable. And controlling the unpredictable was his specialty. He never panicked, never flinched at unforeseen obstacles. Rodman thrown out of a game? *No problem, we'll pick up his rebounds.* Scottie injured? *No problem, we'll handle his points.* Team being dismantled at the end of the season? *I got this. Give me the ball and get out of the way.*

You can't manage any of that if your mind is battling everything else in your life.

His routine allowed him the mental freedom and clarity to focus on one thing: the complexity of the game, and managing every variable that stood between himself and a win. He planned for the unpredictable, and structured his life to minimize the impact it would have on his performance.

But the greats understand you can't plan for everything. Winning respects your routines and habits, but it thrives on the unpredictable, and will keep throwing fastballs—high and inside, sometimes at your head—until it throws the curveball, just to see if you can adapt and handle the unexpected. If you can only do things one way, if you can't operate outside your own system, Winning gets bored and finds someone else to play with.

A routine may allow you to set a portion of your journey on autopilot, but to get to your ultimate destination, you're going to need total control over the outcome. That's the difference between a winning quarterback who can call an audible in a bad situation and turn it into a success, and a failing quarterback who can only execute the play he rehearsed. If you're flying a fighter jet, you can't leave complete control to the autopilot; you must be ready at all times to override the system and handle the unexpected.

Many of us had to face that challenge during the Covid-19 pandemic, which disrupted or altered almost every aspect of our lives in some way. Suddenly, basic routines changed—or disappeared altogether—with limited options to put things back the way they were. All the things that were part of a daily routine—what time you got up, when you left the house, when you went to the gym, where you had lunch, who you saw and spoke to, what time you returned home, what you did when you came in the door, how you relaxed in the evening, what time you went to bed—were suddenly altered or eliminated.

Every routine, every habit, every procedure had to be replanned and relearned. For some, it was a disaster, because they couldn't cope with the rapidly changing landscape. But for others, it was an opportunity to get rid of old habits, break old routines, and find a new way to do things.

For many, it exposed the pointless habits and systems we plug into, over and over, without any real benefit. I used the situation to challenge my clients, especially those in business trying to create a new "normal" for themselves and their teams: Why do you have this routine? For fear? Boredom? Strategy? That's how it's always been done? You don't know another way? What are you limiting by clinging to this? How does it help you win?

For pro athletes who live by the schedule and routine, the quarantines and new protocols presented an interesting challenge. When you play one way your whole career—in front of fans, surrounded by family and friends, on a set schedule that never varies—it takes an extra level of focus to deal with a new reality, from empty stadiums to the NBA bubble. Some handled it with no problems. Others couldn't handle the disruption to their routines, and it showed in their results. The difference wasn't physical. It was all mental.

Every routine has to factor in the possibility of uncertainty. If you prepare only for one scenario, you have no chance of surviving the volatility of real-game conditions. True in sports, true in business, true in life. If you can only function when things are done a certain way, at a certain time, that tells me you lack the ability to adapt to real-time variables.

In basketball, for example, you can practice the perfect shot all you want, but in the game you're never going to know how the pass is coming to you. Over the years, I've thrown countless passes to my athletes, and there were times they'd throw them right back because they didn't like how I threw them. Too high, too low, too hard, too soft, whatever. I once had an intern everyone hated, not because he wasn't great at what he did, but because his passes were too soft. Drove the players crazy. And I understood the intern's issue, because even if you're strong, you probably don't have the strength of an NBA player, and you're throwing a thousand passes a day to these guys, and each player wants the ball at a different height, different location. But every time he'd throw that weak pass, that's what they'd think about, instead of focusing on what they were doing. They wanted to see the ball at game speed.

So I'd throw unpredictable passes on purpose, and when they'd complain I'd tell them: How often in a game are you getting that perfect pass in the perfect location? You have to be able to reach here or there, and be ready for the pass that isn't what you expected. I don't want you, in that moment, thinking, *Oh shit, bad pass!* I want to see you reflexively catch whatever you're thrown.

If a player missed a shot he should have made, we'd work on that by passing him the ball exactly how it had been thrown to him when he missed it, so we could figure out what happened and make sure it didn't happen again.

I used to kill myself with these passes. Most coaches would stand under the basket to rebound the ball and pass it back to the player to take another shot. But in a real game, the pass can come from anywhere. So every time my guys shot the ball, I'd run to the basket, get the ball, run to a different location, pass to him, run back to the basket, get the ball, run to another location, pass to him . . . because that was the precise battle they needed to fight. Not just the physical battle to master the shot, but the mental battle to stay focused when things don't go as planned.

And yes, I could have had an intern or assistant do all the running and rebounding, and sometimes I did. But my top players wanted to see me work just as hard as they did; they needed to know we were going into battle together, and we would win the war together. I can still see the smirk on Kobe's face when he would miss a few shots on purpose just to make my ass run to get the long rebounds.

The battle begins and ends in your own mind. Your thoughts have to be constantly renewed, like a daily subscription that must be paid so you can think clearly. You get updates for your computer and your phone; how often do you update your ideas? Your strategies? Your priorities? How often do you reboot your mental energy and delete the outdated programs and files?

Action originates in your thoughts. Winning will pull you in one direction, but your mind will pull you back: *It's too tough. I didn't expect this. I'm not ready. I'm not good enough.*

Are you confident enough in yourself to win that battle? Are you ready to gamble on yourself to win? We're about to find out.

#1.
WINNING IS THE ULTIMATE GAMBLE ON YOURSELF

The night before I began training Kobe Bryant in 2007, I was sitting in a little restaurant near my hotel in Newport Coast, and Kobe walked in for takeout sushi.

I didn't know him well at that point. We'd talked on the phone numerous times after Michael told him to hire me, and had crossed paths a few times over the years, but we'd never really spent any time together.

That was about to change dramatically.

Over the years, numerous players had asked MJ if they could use me to train them during the season, and always got his standard response: *I don't pay him to train me; I pay him not to train anyone else.* But at this point, he was already retired, and he genuinely wanted to see Kobe play at the highest level for as long as he could.

I'd seen and heard all the comparisons between the two, done my own homework, and was ready to find out for myself how similar or different they actually were.

The first major difference I noticed: Kobe Bryant was

able to walk into a sushi restaurant at dinnertime, and not one person ran over to him for pictures or autographs.

I'm not saying that to be critical or disrespectful, just being factual. Michael could never have done that, ever, and I'd spent so many years around him I'd come to expect that every superstar was treated the same.

Our work together began the next day, at UC Irvine. Kobe was quiet, reserved . . . totally focused. We talked about his knee issues, some other things he wanted to work on, and the one thing that had been on his mind for a long time: He wanted to learn everything he could about MJ. The program, the schedule, the workouts, the whole routine. He wanted to know about Michael's lifestyle, how he reacted to certain situations, how he handled teammates and coaches, and anything else Kobe could add to his arsenal of weapons.

He wanted knowledge.

Not so he could become MJ. So he could become a better Kobe.

Most players who have asked me about MJ over the years are looking for ways to copy his mentality and his game, which can't be done. I can list all the traits and habits and philosophies that made him great, but the secret is in how they're put together, and that's unique to every individual. You can take every ingredient in Coca-Cola—they're listed right on the can—and combine them in a thousand different ways, but you'll never be able to replicate Coca-Cola, because it's not about the ingredients, it's about the formula for combining those ingredients.

When you're iconic, you can never be duplicated.

Kobe understood that. He wanted to learn, so he could

implement certain things that would work for him, and continue to elevate his own game. Because when you're already that good, there aren't many people who can show you how to get better.

I'm often asked about the differences and similarities between the two. I don't like to compare, because to me they were so different and unique that it's an injustice to both. But if you want a basic summary, I'll give you this:

Kobe worked harder. MJ worked smarter.

Kobe never stopped. He questioned me about every aspect of our training; he needed to know why and how everything worked. He didn't always want to be there— *What we got left?*—but he always did the work, and he always came back for more.

He was insatiable for game film. He'd watch a play over and over and over, processing what happened and how he could make it happen better. He carried a DVD player everywhere—this was before iPads—so he could watch special videos made for him by the team. When that wasn't enough, we brought in my director of player development, Mike Procopio, to break down film on every game and every opponent, studying and strategizing for every possible scenario. From 2:00 a.m. to 4:00 a.m., that was Kobe's focus . . . unless he was in the gym putting up shots.

If there was an open gym at 3:00 a.m. and he wanted to work on something, he'd be in that gym. I never slept during those years, I just napped, because you never knew when he'd be ready to get back to work. We'd be on the court at 3:00 a.m., and by 4:30, I'd make him leave so he could get some rest. But I'd stay . . . because I knew he'd sneak back in fifteen minutes, and I'd have to make him leave all over again. Of all the things we worked on, the most challenging was simply getting him to stop.

In athletic performance, everything is about go-go-go and up-up-up, with not enough time and attention paid to STOP. Winning needs you to occasionally stop, land, listen, see, smell, learn, understand. If all you can do is go, you will eventually run right past Winning and not even recognize it.

MJ knew when to stop. He processed things so quickly that he didn't need to study as long and hard; he just knew. He'd look at film but usually just to confirm what he'd already replayed in his mind. His head was like an infinite library of images and moments and plays; he recalled every action and reaction, and knew how to prepare for whatever was ahead.

You'd never find him on a court at 4:00 a.m. He slept at night, because he knew sleep was part of his training, and as I mentioned earlier, we'd work out almost every day at 5:00 a.m., 6:00 a.m., or 7:00 a.m., depending on our schedule and time zone. Occasionally, he'd want to do a late-night training session while we were on the road, just to make sure we got it in. One time he wanted to go straight to the gym when we landed, and I had to borrow a T-shirt from him because I didn't have time to go to my room and change. Two years later, he saw me wearing that T-shirt again and remembered that I never returned it. The man never forgot anything—as we all saw in *The Last Dance*.

He never questioned what we were doing or why we were doing it; he relied on his ability to feel what was working for him. I'd give him the program, and we'd get it done. Usually, he'd have me do it with him, so he'd have someone to compete against. But his goal was to be efficient and effective, as it was with everything.

About those 5:00–6:00–7:00 a.m. workouts: Our entire conversation after games would sometimes amount to me asking him "What time?" and Michael shooting back a number, 5, 6, or 7. But I've never explained why we always switched it up:

Winners need to be at their peak in any situation, regardless of time zone or location or other variables. For you, that might mean getting to a meeting in bad weather with flight cancellations, or a last-minute schedule change that forces you to get up earlier than usual, or something else that throws you out of your comfort zone. For my athletes, it's essential that they perform at the highest level at any time of day, in any time zone. If they're always training at the same time, their bodies get acclimated to one thing, which doesn't work if they're playing all over the country, and especially if they're playing coast-to-coast within a couple of days. So we always vary the times of our workouts so my athletes can be prepared for anything.

While MJ was all about efficiency, Kobe was all about *more*: If some was good, more was better. Michael knew when he'd done enough, so he could move on to whatever was next.

Over the years, I've thought a lot about what made them each so special, and no question, each had immeasurable traits that defined their greatness. Skill and talent, of course. Work ethic. Intelligence. Commitment. Resilience.

But above all, they had this in common: They each possessed an unshakable confidence in themselves that never wavered.

They didn't have to know what was coming, but they were always ready. They knew when to take the shot, and when to pass to someone else. When to talk, and when to stay silent. When to speed up, and when to slow down. When to respond to criticism, and when to laugh it off.

For Michael, it was believing he'd get past the Bad Boy Detroit Pistons and the physical abuse they heaped on him, to become the best who ever played the game. Ignoring the criticism and skepticism when he retired from the NBA after three championships to explore a career in baseball. Ignoring more criticism and skepticism when he returned to the NBA almost two years later, when everyone said he could never be as good, and then winning three more championships. Giving everything he had to the Last Dance Bulls, knowing the team was going to be dismantled at the end of the season.

He never recruited superstars to play alongside him, although the organization was always asking him to do so. At one point, the Bulls management asked him to be part of a conference call with Sam Bowie, who was a free agent at the time. Everyone made their pitch to Sam about why he should join the Bulls, and how much the team wanted and needed him in Chicago. Phil made his pitch, along with Jerry Krause and Scottie . . . and then it was MJ's turn.

"Sam, you comin' or not?" he said. "We're winning with or without you."

His belief in himself was so powerful he never doubted the outcome. Even after he retired, he was still finding ways to invest in himself and his abilities. He bought the Charlotte Hornets and became the first NBA player to be majority owner of a team. He remained an integral part of Nike's Jordan Brand, which earned over $3 billion in 2020. He started—and ran—numerous new ventures and businesses. He competed on golf courses (including the private course he built for himself), he competed in fishing tournaments.

He didn't *have* to do any of that—the man is already worth over a billion dollars.

But Winning is an addiction like none other, and once it shows you some unforgiving love, you'll crave that love forever.

It was no different for Kobe. Everything he did was about his massive belief in himself, starting with his decision to skip college and go right into the NBA. He won three championships alongside Shaq, and then spent the rest of his career proving to himself he could win without Shaq—twice. He learned five languages, including Mandarin Chinese (because he knew the NBA was going to be huge in China) and Slovenian, so he could trash-talk Luka Dončić from the sidelines. He'd speak to Lakers teammate Pau Gasol in Spanish, so none of the opposing players knew what they were going to do. He played through injuries that would have destroyed most players, rupturing his Achilles but staying on the floor long enough to make two free throws, and then asking if there was a way to just "tape it up" so he could keep going.

And after his basketball career, when most players are trying to find ways to cling to their glory days, he went directly into the entertainment business, winning an Oscar for the short film *Dear Basketball* (which he narrated and executive produced) and also writing bestselling children's books. And he shared his love of basketball with a new generation of players, investing his time and passion into coaching his daughter Gianna and other young girls to a standard of excellence most NBA teams couldn't match. I have no doubt he was preparing Gigi to be the first woman to play in the NBA.

That's how you bet on yourself.

For both MJ and Kobe, it all came down to a relentless belief in whatever they did. The same is true of *all* the greats I worked with—Dwyane Wade, Charles Barkley, Tracy McGrady, Scottie Pippen, Hakeem Olajuwon, and so many others. Every decision, every move, was rooted in confidence.

In the early days of Michael's career, a reporter asked his coach Doug Collins about his strategy for coaching the greatest player in the game.

"It's pretty simple," said Collins. "Give him the ball and get the fuck out of the way."

The greats don't need to be told what to do. They already know, and they always find a way to make the gamble pay off.

Very few people are able—or willing—to bet on themselves. They become the assistant manager of their own lives, waiting for directions and approval from some higher authority because they don't feel confident enough to make decisions and take action on their own.

Confidence is the ultimate drug, and Winning is the

dealer. It's the cure for doubt and insecurity and panic and low self-esteem, the antidote to the free fall you experience when you're losing control, the vaccine for fear and weakness. But there's no prescription for it, and no one can give it to you. Either you feel it deep in your gut and bring it out, or you don't.

Whenever we talk about what's "deep inside" us—instinct—I go back to the undisputed experts: babies and little kids. What are we born with, and what are we taught?

We all start out confident. Babies take their first steps, fall down, get up, fall down, laugh, cry, get up, fall down, and they keep going. At no point do they say, *I'm done with this. I'm sitting. Forever.* They do what feels right, and they don't care what you think about it. If they don't like what you've fed them, they'll spit it out. When kids see a puppy, their first reaction is to play with it. It's not until someone teaches them *NO! DON'T! BE CAREFUL!* that they learn hesitation and fear.

Little kids sing and dance for no reason; they draw crazy scribble pictures and dress in whatever feels right to them. They've got one purple boot and one orange sneaker, fairy wings and a hard hat and four T-shirts, and they're singing "Happy Birthday" to everyone on the street.

Until the adults get involved. *You can't wear that! You look crazy! Get in the house! Change your clothes! It's no-body's birthday, why are you singing?!*

And no matter how confident those little kids are, eventually someone shames them out of it. Or something happens to make them believe they're not good enough in some way.

Very few kids have the ability to ignore that, and it stays with you.

Every successful individual can tell you about the humiliating moment (or moments) that defined their level of confidence, and made them choose: Losing or Winning?

For MJ, it was being cut from his high school basketball team. Tom Brady was the 199th pick in the NFL draft. Kobe had his famous "airball game" as an eighteen-year-old rookie in the 1997 playoffs, when he shot an airball at the end of the fourth quarter and then three more in overtime. Dwyane received only three college scholarship offers when he was in high school, and was declared ineligible to play his freshman year at Marquette because of academic issues. Charles Barkley, who weighed three hundred pounds as a rookie, asked teammate Moses Malone why he wasn't getting more playing time, and was told he was too fat and lazy. Scottie Pippen began his freshman season at the University of Central Arkansas as the team equipment manager.

None of us is safe from Winning's sick sense of humor. Just ask the sales rep who falls one deal short of earning her bonus, the NFL kicker who misses the game-winning field goal, the pitcher who blows up in Game 7, the lawyer who loses a huge case on a technicality.

If you're a winner, everything after that becomes a never-ending commitment to keep betting on yourself, a decision about what comes next: *Where do I go from here? Am I this bad? Or am I so much better than this, and now I need to prove it . . . not to everyone else, but to myself?*

For me, there were so many of those moments I can't

recall them all. As a child, I started first grade at age four (I'd just arrived in the United States with my dad, and they took his word for it when he said I was already in first grade), and was immediately put in the class for kids who couldn't keep up with the rest of the class. I couldn't read out loud, and I couldn't spell. We'd have to get up in front of the class and the teacher would give us a simple word:

"Tim, please spell the word 'ham.'"

I thought for a minute. Who cares how you spell ham; you eat it, you don't spell it. But okay: "H . . . A . . . N."

Hilarity all around the class. But I wasn't laughing, and it's still not funny to me, although that story gets a great laugh when I tell it. Those things stay with kids.

Looking back, some of my greatest humiliations were in the classroom, which was so wrong since I always had good grades (in my family, there was no other option). My first year in college as a kinesiology major, I'd talked my way into an advanced class without taking the prerequisite class that would have taught me what I needed to know. The professor started the quarter by having everyone stand, and he'd ask questions of each student. If you couldn't answer, you'd remain standing for the entire class.

I stood for seven and a half weeks, three times a week. Everyone else had answered his questions—they were all sitting. I stood there alone, sweating and embarrassed and furious with myself. Until I realized I could stand there and fail, or I could get the basic kinesiology book and learn what I was supposed to already know.

To this day I remember the moment I answered a question correctly—ironically, it was during the twenty-third class session—and the professor said: "Mr. Grover, you can sit down now."

By then, of course, I'd already taught myself the entire course, and I wouldn't stop answering questions until finally the professor had to say, "Mr. Grover, I don't need you to speak now."

I finally arrived. So did my confidence.

Confidence comes to us in many ways, not just in how we see ourselves, but in how others see us.

A few years ago I was working with a group of CEOs and corporate leaders, as part of a seminar on competitive excellence. Every individual in the room was successful, affluent, and highly respected among colleagues and peers. We were talking about the personal obstacles and issues they'd faced in their race to the top.

"Who here has been told you were worthless?" I asked. A few nervous hands went up.

"Stand up and stay standing," I told them. "Who has been told you're wasting your time?" A few more stood. "This is going to fail. You're never going to make it." More and more standing. And finally: "You're crazy."

By now everyone was standing. "I'm standing here too," I said. "That last part was a compliment. Everyone who has ever accomplished anything has had the confidence to be a little crazy."

Are we talking about you here? Are you working toward things that look crazy to others, but make perfect sense to you? Are you betting on your own belief in your ability and vision, even when everyone else can't see it and wants you to stop?

Don't stop.

Excellence is lonely. No one will ever understand what you've gone through to get where you are.

Of course, you have to have some reason to believe you can achieve what you're going for. You're not going to be the first fifty-year-old NBA rookie, you're not going to win the Masters if you've never won your local neighborhood tournament, you're not going to become a billionaire by just looking at expensive things and wishing they were yours. Every day counts, especially for athletes who have a specific skill set with a tight expiration date. The greats understand the reality of that.

Confidence takes on special meaning when everything is on the line. It's no longer just about walking in a room like you own it, or feeling good in what you're wearing, or knowing all the answers if anyone asks. When you're competing for the prize, when it's all on your shoulders, confidence is all about knowing, without a doubt, that you will win. That was Tom Brady, who left the New England Patriots after winning six championships, decided to play for the Tampa Bay Buccaneers instead, and, at age forty-three, delivered their first Super Bowl title in almost twenty years.

Confident people are their own special breed of killers; you can't break them because they've already been broken, over and over. That's how they became so confident in the first place: not from others telling them how good they are and throwing confetti and parades, but by being pushed down and kicked and laughed at, and by learning for themselves how strong and powerful they really are.

By being in the worst possible situation, and having the confidence to believe: We're getting out of this mess.

Just ask the 2016 Chicago Cubs, who carried the burden of 108 losing seasons into Game 7 of the World Series against the Cleveland Indians. With the game tied and momentum swinging toward the Indians, a sudden storm swept in and forced the game into a seventeen-minute rain delay. Cubs' outfielder Jason Heyward looked around at his teammates, saw them hanging their heads and preparing for the 109th season of defeat, and gave a stern talk that by all accounts lifted up the team and saved the game. His confidence became theirs. That's leadership.

Confidence is feeling as low as you've ever felt in your life, and knowing you'll recover stronger than you were before. It's hearing others tell you everything is fine, you're perfect just the way you are . . . and knowing they're wrong and you still have work to do.

Consider the legendary Phil Heath, seven-time Mr. Olympia, fighting for his eighth title one year after surgery kept him out of competition. He could have walked away, he could have taken his medals and accolades and pursued many other opportunities. But he had the confidence to try again and prove to himself he could still do the work and compete at the highest level, knowing the outcome was not guaranteed.

Confident people don't live in the past; they remember what happened, but they don't let it affect their ability to move forward. They understand that losing is inevitable, and they recover as quickly as possible to get rid of the stink. I don't want to see an athlete slumped over, hiding under his hoodie at a postgame press conference; if you blew it, if you sucked, if it hurts like hell, admit it, own it, and show confidence that it won't happen again. When you're still in the middle of the race, there should be no difference in your demeanor until the race is done.

When you've been knocked down, confidence gives you the patience to stay down for a minute, until you know how to get up better than you were before. Most people jump right back up because they don't want to look weak and damaged, and then immediately get knocked down again. When you're confident in your ability to recover, you know you'll never be weak or damaged again.

We're all flawed. Confident people don't hide their flaws; they laugh at them, because they don't care what you think. Those flaws work for them. They don't have to work for you.

Confidence lets you hear the voices around you and in your own head, without responding or reacting. You can hear them without listening to a single word.

Confidence gives you the grit to stand in the shadow of those more powerful than you, and still retain your power. Every one of my clients was wealthier and more famous than I, and had the power to terminate our relationship at any time. But I never let that influence how I trained them and how I approached our relationship, and I never forgot why I was there: to deliver results that no one else could produce for them. That was my power, and I never gave it up.

Confidence is your ticket to freedom, your escape route from everything that's holding you back. Bad relationships, bad decisions, bad situations . . . the people and issues that stand between you and what you want. Never let anyone take that from you; even when they control the situation, they don't control *you*.

Ultimately, confidence is about taking chances, and never doubting the outcome.

You can't win if you can't gamble on yourself, and you can't gamble if you don't believe you can win.

Winning requires you to set unrealistic goals, and expect to achieve them. That doesn't mean chasing unattainable dreams; it means making smart, educated, and confident decisions about what you're capable of achieving. When you're making those decisions and enjoying the results, life is so short; it feels as if you'll never have enough time to enjoy your wins and create new ones.

But when you're stuck in one place, scared to try something new and feeling trapped in a life you don't really want, every day is endless, and the regret lasts forever.

Taking chances is about embracing the darkness of the unknown. It's about facing reality and fear and uncertainty, because wherever you're going, you're going alone; every hazy step will be uneven, unstable, unpromised. But as you continue to take those steps, as you get closer to Winning, you can see light in the darkness and reality through the haze, until that crazy gamble starts to look like a real possibility. Even when you're the only one who can see it.

People will tell you to "visualize" Winning, to see yourself as a winner. That's not enough. Winning wants you to see, hear, smell, touch, taste, and use your sixth and seventh senses as well, the ones only you know about.

This is your risk to take, no one else's. If you need to be motivated to take that leap, if you keep a list of "20 ways to stay positive," if you're surrounded by people who keep telling you to slow down and roll their eyes every time you talk about your plans . . . you won't get there.

Most people have so many dreams and ideas and abilities they hold on to, unsure and unable to take a chance on themselves, until it's too late, and they die leaving everything unused and untried.

These aren't random gambles, or reckless guesses. They're disciplined choices, about things that matter to you. They're the decisions you have to make if you're going to *experience* your life, not just live it. Are you worth that risk?

If you think the cost is too high, wait until you get the bill for doing nothing.

Every day, you gamble on countless things. What you eat, where you drive, how you speak to people, whom you trust. Everything has risk, everything has consequence. You don't always know the outcome, but Winning does, and it's waiting for you to find out.

#1.

WINNING ISN'T HEARTLESS, BUT YOU'LL USE YOUR HEART LESS

What's your definition of a great teammate?

Supportive? Committed? Dedicated? Responsible?

How about these: Humble? Willing to play any role? Positive attitude?

Those are excellent traits. Absolutely. You need those teammates.

Now here's a slightly different take from Kobe, in an interview about being a teammate:

"If you're going to lollygag through this scrimmage, through this drill, I'm going to beat you, I'm going to let you know I beat you, and I'm going to want you to reconsider your professional life choice. And for the most part, people will say that doesn't make a great teammate. Well, I'm not here to be a great teammate. I'm here to help you win championships."

Not quite the same thing, is it?

Here's a scene from *The Last Dance* in which Michael talks about the same topic:

"My mentality was to go out and win at any cost," he

said. "If you don't want to live that regimented mentality, then you don't need to be alongside of me because I'm going to ridicule you until you get on the same level with me. And if you don't get on the same level, then it's going to be hell for you."

"People were afraid of him," said MJ's former teammate Jud Buechler. "We were his teammates, and we were afraid of him. There was just fear. The fear factor of MJ was so, so thick."

Their Bulls teammate Will Perdue added this: "Let's not get it wrong, he was an asshole. He was a jerk. He crossed the line numerous times. But as time goes on, you think back about what he was actually trying to accomplish, and you're like, 'Yeah, he was a helluva teammate.'"

Hard to overlook those six championships.

I don't think it's a great surprise to anyone that Michael and Kobe were hard on their teammates. Honestly, it would be a bigger surprise if you were reading this book and didn't already know that.

Eleven rings between them. Gold medals. MVPs. MJ was 6-for-6 in the Finals, Kobe was 5-for-7.

You tell me. Could you work with people like that? Could you give it all for someone you could only describe as an asshole? Someone you feared and dreaded seeing every day, knowing the end result will most likely be a win?

I thought so.

Wanting to win isn't the same as knowing how to win. They knew how to win. They put their thoughts ahead of their emotions, ahead of everyone's emotions, and they got it done.

Their minds were stronger than their feelings.

If you want the actual formula, it looks like this: MIND > FEELINGS.

Feel free to use that at your gym or office, on your bulletin board or bedroom ceiling, anywhere you or your team need a reminder.

If you want to understand the mind of a champion, you have to accept that you're dealing with a mind unlike any other. It's going to be rough and intense and dark, and probably intimidating as hell if you're not on that level. And you're going to have to set aside the feelings that go along with that, if you want to compete and achieve your ultimate end result.

If the mind does its job, the right feelings will be there at the end when you win. If not, you end up with feelings no one wants.

The mind of a champion is about controlling as many situations as possible, and controlling the uncontrollable for as long as possible. It might only be for a split second, but that split second can be the difference between everything and nothing.

The higher the pressure, the longer you fight to stay at the top, and the more you focus on this one thing, the less you allow your heart to have a voice in your decisions and actions. You don't have the luxury of being any other way. When you're giving everything you have, making every sacrifice, and devoting every part of your life to Winning, it's hard to tolerate anyone in your circle who isn't doing the same. It doesn't matter if they can't or they won't, your frustration is going to be the same.

They might understand how you feel. They probably won't.

When you're so intensely dedicated to what you're working for, you have to accept that others just won't get it. They don't see what you see, because they can't even imagine what you see.

You're creating so much distance between you and everyone else that they finally stop trying to keep up, and they tell themselves and everyone else that you're just plain difficult. You're obsessed. You're crazy. You're headed for disaster.

You are the problem.

Believe me when I say this: You are *not* the problem. You are the solution. You're already solving problems they can't even see.

I was doing some consulting for a tech company that decided to let go of its top performer because she had a reputation for being "difficult." She didn't get along with everyone, they said; she pushed others too hard and often made people uncomfortable by insisting that everyone needed to do better. Someday maybe I'll understand why that's a bad thing; I'll take difficult and effective over easy and incompetent any day. But there were ego and personality issues, probably because the pressure and tension were too high, and management decided it would be better for "morale" to let her go, along with her huge book of business and years of experience.

And within a month of her departure, morale and productivity actually got worse, because those who had the issues with her suddenly had no one to blame for their poor performances, and no one to hold them accountable. And eventually, her former bosses realized that the person who was the "problem" was actually the one holding it all together. The "thorn" in everyone's side was the most important part of the rose.

A rose with thorns lives longer than a rose with the thorns clipped.

When you stop putting a high value on other people's opinions of you, you give yourself permission to stop caring about the little issues and problems and distractions that fascinate everyone else. It makes you harder and colder, and deadens your feelings and emotions to what others say about you.

Early in MJ's career, critics said he was the reason the Bulls couldn't win. He didn't pass enough, he took too many shots, he didn't trust his "supporting cast," as he called them. That was before his six championships.

Kobe, they said, was a selfish player who didn't elevate his teammates, and wouldn't have won his first three championships without Shaq by his side. He went on to win two more without him.

They were each chasing something, and they weren't going to allow anyone or anything to get in their way. While others were trying to put out brushfires, they were already controlling a raging inferno. *I got this. Let me do what I do.*

Your greatest winners are the least sensitive. And the more they win, the less sensitive they become. LeBron James is a great example of this; earlier in his career, he was far more affected by media and criticism than he is today. That's how the greats handle the noise. They've been through it all; they're hardened to criticism and setbacks. Could MJ have taken the Bulls to their sixth and final title, knowing everything that was happening behind the scenes, if he'd allowed his emotions and feelings to get in the way? No. He played. He dominated. He won.

If he was an "asshole" in the process, he didn't care.

As Michael said in *The Last Dance*: Winning has a price. Leadership has a price.

I've learned over the years that if you want to make people emotional, you should talk about their emotions. I did exactly that in my book *Relentless* and got a lot of people very upset with me. I was talking about getting in the Zone during competition and performance, controlling the uncontrollable, and I wrote: "Emotions make you weak."

I won't repeat the whole discussion here, you can read it yourself, but here was the point: The Zone is about calmness and clarity. Emotions are the complete opposite.

It's true. The more emotional you get, the more you have to deal with those feelings instead of just focusing on what you're doing.

People weren't happy. I heard from parents who told me kids need to be able to show emotion. I heard from psychologists who said this is what's wrong with society, everyone is afraid to show emotion. I heard from coaches who said they want their teams playing with emotion.

Folks: I'm not against emotion. We are not robots. I want you to laugh and cry and be happy and sad and happy again.

Just not all at the same time, especially while you're trying to win.

To the coaches, I will add this:

Stop telling your teams to play with emotion. Emotions are volatile and unpredictable and erratic, especially when you have multiple emotions bubbling up at the same time. You don't want them playing with emotion. You want them playing with energy. Huge difference.

Go ahead and tell a team you want to see emotion. What does that mean, exactly, to each individual? Which emotions do you want to see? You want them to laugh? Cry? Curl up and be scared? Do you want to see joy in the middle of the game while you're losing? Sadness? Fear? Confusion? Hurt? Embarrassment? You really want any of those in your game? Those are all emotions. None are going to help you win.

You want energy. Focus. Intensity. You want to be alert and aggressive and strong. None of those are emotions, they are a state of mental power. You want your mind locked in, so you don't even feel the nerves and pressure that come with competition. Emotional screaming and yelling doesn't make you a winner. It just makes you loud and distracting.

I'm not saying you shouldn't laugh or have fun or get excited about a big moment, go ahead. But only for the moment; you must be able to restore calm and clarity in an instant, because you don't know what the next moment is going to bring.

And if you're going to play with emotion—because it works for you and you have the results to prove it—then make sure you're playing with *one* emotion, steady and consistent. Take the roller-coaster highs and lows out of it. You must remain steady and focused regardless of how you feel. Your mind must remain stronger than your feelings.

After you win, or lose, there's plenty of time to be emotional about whatever happened. But during competition, the only thing you should feel is total control. It's your responsibility to demand that of yourself.

Not easy, I know. Every day, Winning does its best to mess around with your mind and feelings, just to throw you off course.

Your mind makes decisions. Feelings ask, *Really? You sure about that??*

Your mind tells you to get to the gym. Feelings say, *Stay in bed. One day won't matter.*

Your mind deals with pain by finding ways to stop hurting. Feelings thrive on being hurt.

Your mind counters the disappointment of failure with the knowledge that it's possible to try again. Feelings cling to regret for everything you never tried.

Your mind manages pressure. Feelings turn pressure into stress, and manage none of it.

Your mind can let go of the past, forgive grudges, and look to the future. Feelings hold on to every last bit of trash, forever.

Weakness, laziness, frustration, negativity, anxiety. Every single morning you get to decide whether to give those things a vote. Do you listen to them? Or do you have the self-control to say: *No. No discussion. Put your hand down, you don't have a vote today.* That's what self-control is: deciding which part of you gets a vote. Some days, frustration might have something to say. Weakness might over-power you. You might give in to jealousy, or laziness, or fear. It happens. Everyone has lapses, we all lose control at some point. But not every day. The skeletons in your mental closet do not get a vote every day. Put those hands down.

Staying in control of yourself is a choice. Losing control is a choice. But to develop that level of control you have to understand what's dictating your actions, and your thoughts. Is it you? Is it something external? Are you so busy fighting with everyone else that you don't even realize your biggest battle is with yourself?

Self-control means facing the things you don't want to face, looking for answers in yourself and not others, knowing you're not always going to be happy or secure. It means resisting the celebration every time something good happens, and not falling apart every time things don't go your way. It's about managing the low moments, the setbacks, and not getting caught up in things you shouldn't—the things that test you.

What happens when you're faced with a situation that challenges you? You have your initial emotional reaction—unhappiness or fear or anxiety, or whatever you're feeling—and then you get the inevitable bonus waves of emotion as you think and think and think about it. The more you think, the more you pull in additional conflict, drama, chaos, until you're so far from the original situation it hardly matters anymore because you now have all these new emotions to deal with.

You can't always control what happens to you, but you can always control how you react. When there's craziness all around you, when everyone is in your ear telling you what to do, you have to remain the maestro of what's going on in your head. Every voice you hear creates a different feeling and a different emotion, and it's up to you to keep them all in line. If you react to everything someone says to you or about you, you're always going to lose.

You want the formula for this? I'll make it easy for you:

- Control your thoughts, and you control your emotions.
- Control your emotions, and you control your actions.
- Control your actions, and you control the outcome.

That's it. Your thoughts create emotions. Your emotions drive your actions. Your actions determine the outcome.

You have to know when to turn your heart off, and your mind on. You must be able to lose your way, and find your way back. Winning wants to see your return ticket, not a one-way trip on a runaway train to failure.

If you're in that gym with MJ, you can either feel the sting of his words and use them to elevate your performance, or you can feel the sting of his words and crumble.

When control is taken from you, focus on the things you *can* control, instead of the things you *can't*. That was the driving force behind MJ's final run with the Bulls: *Coach isn't coming back, the team is being broken up, you've taken away our control over what happens next. I can't argue with you about bringing the coach back, you made your decision to break up the team, fine. But I still control how we play. So I will control the one thing I can: Winning.*

You can control showing up. You can control pushing yourself harder. You can control not complaining. You can control not giving a fuck. You can control being there.

During the Covid-19 pandemic, I just about lost my mind every time I heard from an athlete who said he or she had no way to work out. Your facility is closed, you have no control over that, I get it. You have a basement? A yard? A field? We will control the things we can control.

What are you willing to control, what will you allow to control you?

Every single time MJ stepped on the court, there was at least one player on the other team determined to get under his skin, because they knew if they could get rid of him, if they could get him to lose control of his emotions, throw a punch, or do something to get thrown out of the game, their odds of winning went way up. Reggie Miller, Danny Ainge, John Starks, Greg Anthony, Dennis Rodman, Danny Ferry, Xavier McDaniel . . . just a few who took their best shot and got the reaction they were looking for. It wasn't easy to do—he didn't have a single ejection in his entire career, and he only fouled out eleven times—but he was definitely willing to get physical when provoked. And then he'd immediately regain control, because there was no way he was going to allow an emotional outburst to impact the outcome of the game.

The most common emotion I see in my athletes and top-tier business clients is anger, because they're so driven and competitive. If that's your fuel, if that's what sets you on fire and launches you into the Zone where nothing can touch you, then you should use it. But as with all explosives, this fuel comes with a warning: "CAUTION: DO NOT USE WITHOUT EXTREME SKILLS, INTELLIGENCE, AND EXPERIENCE."

Performing with anger can work for you if (a) it's your natural response to competition, and (b) you know how to control it. Otherwise, you're going to lose control in the heat of the moment, without the ability to control what follows.

It takes no control to clench a fist. It takes a lot of control to open it and walk away.

I never had any of my athletes box as part of their training, because I didn't want to them thinking about taking swings at people.

A coach who screams at his team "*Play mad!*" is asking for a chaotic mess, unless the athletes are accustomed to playing that way. If they haven't developed the mental skills and control to handle that kind of turbo, it's like giving a kid the keys to the Lamborghini. It won't end well.

I have my own scale for measuring anger, because all anger isn't the same. You start with calm, and move to annoyed, mad, pissed off, angry, and finally enraged. Calm gives the most control, enraged takes all control away.

When you're annoyed or mad, you might not take action; you can keep it all internal. By the time you're pissed off, those feelings are starting to show. Anger leads you to the edge of losing control, and if you've reached enraged, you've lost it completely.

Ideally, you learn how to create controlled rage, where you can be calm and aggressive at the same time.

Most people go straight to anger. And if you can't manage annoyed, mad, and pissed, anger is going to burn right through you and escalate to rage. But rage isn't sustainable: That kind of intense energy and emotion burns quicker and flames out faster. If you didn't get your results in those first few moments, you're done. You've lost your advantage. You get a huge explosion, your tank drains to empty, your fuel is gone, and you look around thinking, *Wait a minute, where was I?*

If you can't control an ordinary car at 30 mph, how are you going to control a high-performance automobile going 180?

The greats understand how to drive that automobile. They can downshift and pump the brakes as easily as they step on the gas; they have the skill and experience to handle that kind of velocity. You might not even be able to see what they're feeling under the surface. Dwyane Wade played some of his best basketball when he was angry, and it never showed. Anyone can see blood, very few can smell it. Wade could, and it took him to another place. But he kept everything internal, and used it for fuel.

Most people can't do that, whether they're competing in sports or business or anything else. They have that one reckless moment of uncontrolled emotion, and they realize a split second too late that they can't get it back.

Motivational talkers and coaches constantly tell you to *Go, go, go. Let's go! Get up and go! It's go time!* Okay, where the fuck are we going?? As I said earlier, no one teaches you to stop. Stopping allows you to learn. Adapt. Focus. Calculate. Strategize. It puts your mind back in control and gets your feelings in check. Everyone tells you to do more. But more isn't always better. Sometimes it's just more of what you don't really want.

Kobe was at his best when I could get him to stop. You need to work out less, and sleep more, I told him. Too many people around Kobe feared him, and didn't want to address this issue, but it was essential to keep him performing at the highest level. Everyone saw him as a relentless workout guy, and he was. But when we were able to curtail some of that, control it, that's when he really started to excel at an even higher level.

A lot of people thought of Kobe as a "control freak." I disagree. To me, that says you're trying to control things you shouldn't, instead of letting others with greater skill and ability do what they do best. Kobe knew when he needed help, and he had no problem asking for it. He hired me, and he brought in many other top professionals as well. But I understand why people thought of him that way; when you're in charge, when you need to stay in charge, it's hard to let go of that mentality.

If you consider yourself a "control freak" in your work or personal life, I urge you to take a hard look at whether that's a good thing. In most cases, it's not. People who demand total control—and get anxious and angry when they can't have it—usually end up shortchanging themselves and everyone around them.

When it comes to working with my clients, I don't want an athlete or his dad or an agent telling me which exercises we should be doing. If I listen to their "suggestions," we have little chance of success. Let me do what

I do, that's why you brought me in. At the same time, I know when to yield control to those who can do things better. I used to do everything for my athletes: physical therapy, massage, skill work, training, nutrition . . . anything they needed. But at some point, I got smarter and realized there were professionals who were more expert in some of those areas. Better for the client, better for all of us.

Winning wants to take your control. It wants to get you emotional and crazed and so excited you can't think straight, so it can get you out of the race faster.

But if you want to stay in that race, if you want to keep your inner fuel burning at optimum level, you have to stay in control of yourself. It's not about talent—you can have tremendous talent and have no self-control. It's about keeping your mental engines cool, no matter how hot things get around you.

#1.

WINNING BELONGS TO THEM ...
AND IT'S YOUR JOB TO TAKE IT

In 1993, Michael Jordan agreed to an interview with CBS's Connie Chung, during which she asked if he had a gambling problem.

"No," he said, laughing. "I can stop gambling. I have a competition problem, a competitive problem . . ."

Not a single person who has ever known MJ would disagree with that.

I learned this the day he hired me. He was my first pro client; I was working as a trainer in a health club, making $3.35 an hour with a master's degree, and decided to send letters to every player on the Bulls offering my services. Every player, that is, except Michael Jordan, because I figured he'd be the last guy who would want to hire a trainer. And of course, he was the *only* guy who wanted to hire a trainer. He was the best player in the league, but he still hadn't made it to the Finals, and he realized he couldn't physically withstand the bigger and stronger players who were killing him on the court. He wanted to compete at an even higher level, and he was willing to do the extreme work to make that happen. He saw my letter in another player's locker, and had the team doctor call me.

After three months of interviews with the Bulls' doctor and head athletic trainer, I was given an address and told to show up the next day. I was not told which player had requested to meet me, and I was so grateful for the opportunity that I didn't want to blow it by asking. But I had sent fourteen letters, and I had fourteen different plans laid out for all the players it could possibly be.

I get to the house, ring the bell . . . and Michael Jordan opens the door. The one player I never planned on seeing.

He's in full Nike gear. He looks down at my shoes. Converse. He stares at them and shakes his head.

So I pull off the shoes—wondering if maybe I should offer to set them on fire—and realize there's a hole in my sock. I put the shoes back on. He's just watching. Says nothing.

We met for an hour, I explained what I could do for him, and he said, "This doesn't sound right."

I answered: "It don't get any righter."

He agreed to give me thirty days, and told me to get whatever equipment we'd need because we'd be working out at his house. I started mentally calculating how long it would take to locate the right weights and machines, get them ordered, shipped, and installed. Remember, this was 1989, before online shopping; you had to physically go to stores to buy the equipment, or order from a catalog. At best, it could take a week, maybe longer.

I asked when he planned to get started.

"Tomorrow," he said, ending the meeting.

As I walked out, he took one last look at those Converse on my feet. "Never again," he said, and shut the door.

From that moment, everything I did was about making both of us better every day. His body, his game, my skills and knowledge. My shoes. The competition never ended, whether you were the other team, the other players, the other shoe companies. For me, it was an instant competition to see how fast I could get his gym set up—yes, we were ready to go that next day—and how I could deliver those results in the next thirty days. I did, and those thirty days turned into fifteen years.

Keeping up was essential if you were part of MJ's world. You didn't only have to keep up with his mentality and drive, he expected you to keep up in your knowledge, your skill, your pace, your desire to win. That was non-negotiable. The first time I traveled with him, it was during the off-season, and he was taking his entire personal team: He had his security, his advisors, a couple of close friends, and of course, his trainer. He told us all to meet at his house, and we'd travel to the airport from there, driving our own cars.

MJ jumps into one of his high-performance automobiles—I think it was a Ferrari—and says to everyone, "You better keep up."

I'm in my father's 1987 Sterling. Not the fastest car ever made, but somehow I manage to pull up at the same time he did; there was no way I was going to fall behind. I drove on the shoulder, ran on and off exit ramps . . . anything I could do to keep him in my sights. I don't recommend this, I'm just telling you what happened. Everyone else was five minutes late. And of course, he let them hear about it.

When they pointed out that no one could keep up with him on the road, he pointed at me and said, "Timmy kept up."

Note to readers: Don't ever call me Timmy. No one else gets to do that.

Keep up. That was his directive for everyone around him, in everything he did. He never had to say it, but we all knew: *We don't compromise, we don't take shortcuts, we don't make excuses. Keep up with me and my standards, or you're out.*

I could tell you hundreds of stories about his competitive nature, his relentless drive to win at everything, over and over. You can find thousands of videos and books and historians who will tell you what they witnessed over the years, as he pursued victory in everything.

But this is one of my favorite examples, probably because no one else knows it.

During the Jordan/Bulls era, my Chicago gym was packed every summer with dozens of elite competitors who came from all over the world for one thing: our legendary pickup games. We'd have dozens of NBA All-Stars and future All-Stars, rookies, and NBA refs, playing on all four courts. They'd work out with us, get some training and coaching and whatever else they needed. But the main attraction was the opportunity to get on the court with MJ.

One very hot, steamy day, we had a new guy who was trying extremely hard to impress everyone, especially Michael. He gets a little overheated and collapses in the middle of a game, right on the floor. Apparently, he'd had about five Red Bulls, and now he's having a seizure. He's foaming at the mouth, sweating profusely, and I can't find a pulse.

We call 911, clear the court, and I'm giving him CPR while we wait for an ambulance.

And while I'm pumping this guy's chest and making sure he doesn't die on my floor, I feel someone stand over me watching what's happening.

MJ.

"I think he's having a heart attack," I tell him.

"Evidently," he says.

At that moment, the guy opens his eyes, slowly sits up, looks around, and sees Michael Jordan standing over him.

He's embarrassed but at least he's breathing.

Michael looks down and says, "Is he okay?"

"He's alive," I say.

"You good?" Michael asks him.

The kid looks up and smiles weakly, a little groggy, but he says, "Yes, sir, I'm good."

"Good," says MJ. "Get a sub," he says to me, "I got a game to win."

That's a competitive problem.

But if you're going to be the greatest of all time, at anything you do, it's reasonable—and essential—to also be the most competitive.

No excuses, no apologies. If that feels extreme to you, you're correct. Extreme results require extreme competition.

Because when someone else has what you want, you need to go get it.

If you consider yourself a highly competitive person, if you never turn it off and never slow down, if others say you're crazy and obsessed and it's all too much . . . I challenge you to be okay with that. I challenge you to keep competing with the same confidence and commitment that has taken you this far. When others talk about your competitiveness like it's a bad thing, remind yourself they can't relate to how you feel, because they've never felt it. That's their loss. It should not be yours.

You can control those competitive urges. But why should you have to?

Winning has no loyalty to you. No matter how long you've battled to become a winner, it takes one split second to become a loser. I know that's a hard reality for a lot of people. They work so hard to get somewhere, and in an instant, it's gone. They gave it up. Or more likely . . . someone took it.

These are the people who won something—once—and never won anything again, because they were so content and overwhelmed by their one big win that they stopped competing for anything else. They still talk about their high school football championship, or the car they won in the sales contest seven years ago. Since then? Nothing. Still talking.

Then there are the "winners" who finally reached their goals, got the big house, four cars, splashy vacations . . . and thought it would last forever. It doesn't. Someone else watched what they did, and did it better. Winning loves to watch someone else kill your dream.

You had a great month? Good for you. See you in thirty days. Someone will be there winning. It might not be you.

And there are also those who love to compete for anything, anytime, but without any real focus or objective. They love the chase, but don't invest the time or skills to catch what they're chasing. So they go after everything, and never really get ahead in anything. But they're "competitive."

Make a note: Being competitive and being a winner aren't the same thing.

Even at the highest level, you're a champion until someone else takes that title . . . and they almost always do. You don't get to keep it. You can keep the memory, a piece of hardware, a few other souvenirs . . . but you can only be a winner when you're winning. As soon as you lose, you give it all back. And Winning gives your seat to someone else.

So if that matters to you, then you have to fight like hell to keep it, and never, ever, take one minute of it for granted.

Great competitors appreciate the trophies and plaques and rings, but those aren't the souvenirs they remember most. They're more likely to recall the bloody scalps of their opponents, the lonely decisions and damaged relationships and divorce papers, the receipts from three hundred nights a year on the road and phone messages they never returned. The rings are beautiful. The war was ugly.

When you're competitive, you know you earned that ring, but it's not enough. Can you get another? And another? Tom Brady, on which of his seven Super Bowl rings is his favorite: "The next one."

Kobe was wired the same way. As I've said, even after his Lakers won three titles in a row, in 2000, 2001, and 2002, on a team that included future Hall-of-Famer Shaquille O'Neal, all he heard was "Yeah, but he had Shaq." The loudest voice was in his own head. *Can I do it without Shaq?* He had to know; he had to have *more*. That's how great competitors get to the next level: They look at what they've accomplished and can't rest until they've done it even better.

Eight years later, after he'd won his fourth and fifth ring (both without Shaq), Kobe was asked in the postgame press conference what that fifth ring meant to him. He didn't talk about his legacy, or his place in history, or the hard work that went into earning those rings. With his two little girls on his lap, he smiled and said: "I just got one more than Shaq," he said. "You can take that to the bank." Then he paused and added: "You know how I am, I don't forget anything."

If that resonates with you, I'm guessing you've competed and won, and you know that gorgeous feeling of beating a rival, a competitor, a colleague, a friend . . . yourself. You know what it feels like to overtake someone and keep going like they weren't even there. You don't look back at what you left behind. All you can see is Winning, looking amused and nodding at you with approval.

But if you haven't experienced this, if you feel like you're not competitive enough, if you worry that there's something missing in you, if you're not seeing results . . . you need to hear this: The ability to compete is in all of us.

You compete for something every minute of the day, with every decision you make. At the basic level, you compete with daily obstacles: *Should I go to the gym? Should I skip this donut? Can I get out of the house on time? Will I get my work done today?*

That's where it starts; if you can't win at those things, you're not going to win at anything else. If you're trying to quit drinking, but every weekend you still go out for a drink, you lose every weekend. The right decisions take you to the next level, closer to Winning. The wrong decisions keep you exactly where you are.

When you can win those small victories, you can start competing for more: *I need to increase the intensity of my workout. I want to lose fifteen pounds. I'm going to get to the office early so I can get more done. I'm going to deliver more than I was asked to.*

Every day, you need to compete at a higher level than the day before. Small decisions. Little changes. New challenges. Bigger ambitions. You're not going to make a million bucks or build your empire or win a championship in one day. You're going to compete for it every day for infinite days. That's how you become not just a competitor, but a true competitor: You get better every day for a long time. Not accidentally, but intentionally.

And you surround yourself with people who do the same. I'm not talking about your "good friends" or the cheerleaders who give everyone a "Woohoo!" and a fist bump on their texts. I'm talking about rock-solid allies you can always count on. Friends will tell you what you want to hear. Allies tell you what you need to hear. Allies elevate themselves to elevate everyone else. They don't have to be your friends—hell, they don't even have to like you—but they share your vision and your goals and thirst for the same result. These are the "ride or die" partners who never ask why or how much; they already know, and they'll take a bullet for the cause. You don't have to ask "How was your weekend?" because you know they spent it the same way you did: figuring out ways to get better.

That was how Dwight Howard unwittingly allowed Kobe and Shaq to rebuild their relationship: It wasn't until Kobe played alongside Dwight that he came to really appreciate Shaq as a teammate, an ally, and a competitor.

When you deliver greatness, you never have to talk about it. Allies don't make excuses, and won't listen to yours. It's not enough to come up short and say, "Well, we worked so hard. We gave it our best." Winning wants you to say nothing, and just show the results.

Great competitors communicate with the fewest words possible. A look. A glare. They don't react to hype or cheerleading. I don't know about you, but I get tired of all the motivational drill sergeants who talk down to people as if they're simpletons: *You gotta want it! Go get it! This is your time! Outwork the competition! Stay up late! Get up early! Fight! Kill! Own it!*

Did you not know any of that?

If someone is preaching to you on that level, it's because they don't think you'll understand straight talk about what competition really feels like. They may not even know. It's not about jumping up and down or hollering or "getting pumped up." That's low-level BS. It works for a moment.

I've heard coaches at the highest pro level talk to their players like they're still in grade school. "Play for the name on the front of the jersey, not on the back! Leave it all on the field! We need to play all sixty minutes!" You've been hearing those things since you were riding your bike to play at the local park. If you're a professional athlete— even if you're still in college—you should never have to hear them again.

If I ever once spoke to any of my clients that way, they'd laugh in my face and then bounce me out of the gym.

As we've discussed earlier, competition isn't about getting loud and vicious and excited. You can be the kindest, most gentle person in world, and still be competitive in every way. This is about quiet desire. Hunger. Adrenaline. Pain. Fatigue. Envy. Pressure. So much pressure.

We all know what it feels like to be hit by a wave of hunger and envy, when you see someone living your dream, enjoying what you want. Some people say it makes them more competitive, to watch someone else achieve the goals they'd set for themselves. If that works for you, let it work. But anger and jealousy are small-time, petty emotions. You have to convert them into action to create results.

We waste so much time talking about how we're going to win that we forget the most important thing: actually winning. There's a big difference between hanging motivational slogans on your wall, and actually doing what those slogans tell you.

You can "want it" and "outwork" everyone. But unless you can deal with the obstacles and hurdles and setbacks, unless you have a plan for dominating the end result, you'll still be wanting it for a long, long, time.

Competition isn't just about the grind, it's about grinding for results. It's about doing work that actually works. Everyone talks about the grind, grinding it out, keep grinding. Well, you can grind and grind and grind, and what's left at the end? Dust. Grinding deforms, it obliterates. Excellence is about sculpting, creating something magnificent that wasn't there before by artfully changing its shape and form. When you sculpt, you strategically remove the parts you don't need, the elements that get in the way. It's the equivalent of not just working hard but working smart.

What are you creating, what's the shape you want it to take?

We're all hardwired to win. It's basic survival. Take a bottle or pacifier from a baby. Beat a little kid in a race or board game. Give something to one child and not to his sister. Very few will just look the other way; we want what we want, and we'll fight you to get it. You can see it in toddlers: What's the first thing they do when they don't win? They throw a block at your head. Hit you with a hockey stick. Storm off in a tantrum. No one likes to lose. It feels unnatural. Winning feels good. It feels like a right. Like you deserve it. You're capable of having it.

I hear from parents all the time who ask how to make their child more competitive. They're worried because their five-year-old doesn't want to play baseball, or chase the other kids around the playground, and they think that's going to translate into a lifetime of passive failure. They want to teach their child to "want it."

Some of those parents are ultra-competitive themselves, and can't understand why their kids aren't the same. They've achieved at such a high level that they can't accept their own children not having that same fire and obsession.

Others are parents who've never won anything, and want a second chance through their kids. They can't win on their own, so they push the kids to deliver on dreams the parents never achieved. They'll invest everything they have in their child's sport or activity in the hope that the kid will be good enough to get a college scholarship . . . whether that's the child's dream or not. These parents all want desperately to know: How do you "teach" competitiveness?

You don't teach it. You can inspire it, you can set an example, you can talk about expectations. But you can't teach someone to want something. Winning is all about you. You can't compete—you can't feel that desire and focus and hunger—for something you don't really want. And you can't want it for someone else. It's the same false sense of "motivation" we discussed earlier, the sugar high. You can tell someone "Let's go!" over and over, but unless they know where you're going, it's a pointless trip. Those kids may not want the thing you're forcing them to pursue, hovering over them, trying to get them "fired up."

But just wait until they lose something they really *want*. You'll see the fire. True for kids, true for your teammates or the people on your staff. The drive to compete can only be as strong as the desire for the end result.

When you lose the fire to fight for something—or if you never had it in the first place—it's because you don't really care about the outcome of the fight. Maybe you're doing it for someone else, or maybe you want so many different things you can't focus on just one. But when you find the thing you truly want to compete for, you'll fight with everything you have to own it, protect it, and keep it.

Competition tells you what you really want. It responds to your desires, your emotions, your instinctive craving, so much that you'll crawl through hell and back to get the thing you crave. You don't even have to think about it, you just know: *That is mine.*

The reality of competition is this: To achieve at the highest level, you have to crave the end result so completely that nothing else matters. And you have to crave it for yourself, not for anyone else. You can't lose weight for anyone else, you can't build a business for anyone else, you can't win a championship for anyone else. If it doesn't burn within you to do it, you can't succeed. If your business is stagnant, if your results are weak, if you're not growing toward your goals and potential, there may be a reason that's not what you think it is.

Because when you find that challenge you truly want to compete for, nothing and no one will be able to stop you.

#1.

WINNING WANTS ALL OF YOU; THERE IS NO BALANCE

When my daughter was around five years old, she was watching me pack for a long road trip, and she asked: "Daddy, why do you have to travel so much?"

"This is how I take care of our family," I told her. "I travel for my work so I can take care of you and Mom and put food on the table."

She was quiet for a moment. And then she said the words that stung me harder than anything that has ever been said to me:

"If I eat less, can you stay home more?"

I had to look away so she didn't see her dad in tears.

It took me nearly thirteen years before I could tell that story without losing it, and even as I write this . . . well, it still hits me hard.

I suppose in a movie the dad would have this thunderbolt moment and decide to never travel again. He'd never miss a school play or a volleyball game, he'd never have to call home from across the world to say "Happy Birthday!" to his little girl.

I kept packing.

Of course, I hugged her and told her I'd be back soon, and we talked about the great things we'd do when I returned. And we did them all.

But on that day, I kept packing.

How do you explain to a five-year-old, or to anyone for that matter, that they're the most important thing in your life, but for right now, this other thing over here is all you can think about?

If you've never felt that sick feeling of disappointing someone because you're consumed with your own goals, you've never experienced the intoxication of Winning.

Winning wants all of you. It doesn't recognize love or sentiment, it doesn't care about your other responsibilities and commitments. It demands obsession, or it will find someone else to consume.

For me, that obsession is my commitment to my clients. Being there when they need me, and even when they don't know they need me. Asking them questions no one else will ask. Working as hard as they do, and sometimes harder. And in my line of work, that means being where they are, anywhere in the world. It means studying everything they do, how they move, how they feel. It means obsessing about how to be .0001 percent better.

It means having to sometimes disappoint a five-year-old.

It hurts me to write that, but we're about to talk about the sacrifices and choices we make when we're chasing our goals, and I'd be lying if I told you it was easy. It's not.

I have no problem admitting my work takes most of

my time and focus and mental energy. This is who I am. It allows me to win and helps my clients win as well. It's up to you to determine how much you're willing to give up to catch what you're chasing.

Your obsession might be your business. Or your sport. Or your talent. Maybe you're focused on losing weight or building your body, or completing your education, or managing your family. Whatever you're trying to accomplish, you know you can't do it without laser focus and total commitment to the end result.

Is there a price to pay for that? Yes. Absolutely.

When you're driven to achieve something that requires all your time, all your focus, all your heart . . . it's extremely difficult to create meaningful space for anything else. You can't achieve balance in all areas of your life.

I know this topic makes many people uneasy, because very few are willing to admit to that degree of obsession. They feel selfish. Neglectful. Guilty about their own choices. They start questioning their priorities. But the more you hide it, the more you pretend you can handle everything and "have it all," the less chance you have of having anything at all.

Anytime I bring this up, especially during a live speech to a big group, I'll have two or three people come up to me afterward—privately, never during the Q&A session—to confide in me about the lack of balance in their lives, like it's their dirty secret. They don't want anyone to know they're neglecting their families or their health or their other commitments. They know what others are saying behind their backs, and to their faces: *Remember me? All you do is work. It's too much! You have no time for anything! You need to slow down! We never see you. When is this going to end?*

You're supposed to work out, but not be "obsessed." You're supposed to work, but not be a "workaholic." You're supposed to do everything others want you to do, but still "have balance."

The voice in your head can be equally harsh: *I need more time for the family. I need to work out. I need to lose weight. I need a vacation. I have a list of two hundred chores. I always told myself I'd write a book. Is this all worth it anyway?*

Listening to all these voices is like following Google Maps, Waze, and MapQuest at the same time. Everyone is giving you different directions, with different arrival times. Fact: If you're trying to get to all those destinations at once, you won't arrive at any of them.

Instead of feeling focused, you feel panicked, chaotic, out of control, and so overwhelmed you can't accomplish anything. You're trying to put energy into everything, and you feel like a total failure because you can't do it all, at least not successfully. You're distracted and angry, and you blame everyone else for demanding so much of you and making this all so difficult. It feels like there's some invisible enemy holding you back and throwing immovable obstacles in your way.

There is no invisible enemy. That enemy is you.

It's as if you're trapped in a room, cluttered with all the responsibilities and commitments you've been hoarding. You want to fill that room with your achievements and success, and instead it's a mess of broken promises. You plan to clean it up, get back in control, but the chaos is so overwhelming you can't even find the door.

And instead of succeeding at the one thing that could make a serious difference, the thing that could make you a winner and allow you to take everyone else with you—give you financial freedom, and finally create more time for everything—you look up at Winning with a sorry shrug and say, "Can't make it. I'm too busy."

Time for everything equals time for nothing. And winning at nothing.

Winning wants all your time and attention; it needs to be the only thing on your mind, 24/7. It might reluctantly allow you to spend a brief time on other things, as long as you return quickly, and never stop thinking about where Winning wants you to be. You might physically be somewhere else, but mentally, you never leave.

So when you tell me you want to be relentless, you want to win, you're obsessed with success, but you also want more balance in your life, I have to give you the truth:

There *is* no balance for those who are committed to Winning. Stop fighting it, stop feeling guilty about it, stop looking for it. And start creating a life on your own terms that works for you and your goals so everyone can win.

If it makes you feel any better, you're not alone if you think you're lacking in ability to balance all the parts of your life. It's the most common issue among my business clients. While athletes have a season that begins and ends—allowing them to unplug and refresh for a couple of months—most people don't have two or three months to shut down and restore balance in their lives; there's no off-season. The work goes on and on and on. The race never ends.

A sense of balance is personal, and it's different for everyone. You don't find it by trying to make everyone happy; you create it by taking a hard look at what you really want, and what it will take to have that in your life. *Your* life, no one else's. If you're worried about what's "normal," what others will think and whether they'll approve, you're done. Keep fitting in. Winners stand out.

It's like having a custom-made suit. You want this fabric, those buttons, that lining, and the pants should be this long. To you, it's the hottest suit ever made. Then someone else looks at the suit and comments: *Why would you get that lining? Are the pants a little long? I wouldn't get that color.* Well, maybe you wouldn't, but I would. Get your own damn suit, this one is perfect for me.

Look, I want you to have success and still have time for family and friends and relaxation and fun. I want you to be there for your kids, they need you. I want you to have a happy relationship with a partner who wants the same things you do. I want it to be easy and organized, and I want everyone to stop being disappointed and angry at you. Most of all, I want you to stop being angry at yourself.

But I also want you to have your goals and your dreams, and I want you to *win*. And to have all of that, something will have to give, for now.

You can't have it all at the same time, and you'll have to get used to the reality that certain things will have to wait. But what's the first thing people do when they feel their

life is unbalanced? They start adding. *I should get a dog.
I need to do more charity work. I have to help my friends
move. I'm supposed to go to this party.*

Now they don't have time for the one thing they really
want, so they have to give up other things just to keep up.
*I'll sleep less. I can get up at 3 a.m. I'll work out before
dawn. I'll stay up extra late and work all night. I can get
it all done.*

No, you can't.

You have to master the art of NO.

"No" is a complete sentence, it requires no interpreta-
tion, and everyone around the globe understands what it
means. They might not like what it means, but they understand it.

And every time you say yes, every time you say maybe
or not right now when you really want to say no, Winning
rolls its eyes and looks at someone else.

Why is it so hard to say no? I know, you want to help
people, you want to be nice, you want to show that you
can take on everything and make it all work. But Winning
doesn't need you to do any of those things. Winning needs
you to win.

I've had clients make a "NO List" of things they are
not going to do, a nonnegotiable reminder of things that
aren't a priority. Keep it in your phone, on your desk, tape
it to the mirror, the refrigerator, and use it. Just making the
list will give you a fresh perspective on what really matters,
and what's just cluttering up your schedule and your life.

Stop adding. Start deleting.

Winning demands total focus. Everything and everyone doesn't merit equal time and attention. If you're going to have more time for what you want, you're going to have less time for the friends who need to fill you in on their daily life dramas, the group texts with thirty people who think it's their job to entertain the group all day, the colleagues who love to have meetings that resolve nothing.

"It's important," they say. *Not to me*, you think.

Delete.

Is it easier to climb a mountain with a weighted vest and a full pack, or with just the essentials? Instead of giving yourself more to do, start getting rid of everything that's dragging you down, everything you're doing to meet other people's expectations and demands. Those things have to go. Handle that, and you already have more time for the meaningful, important elements in your life: family, kids, health . . . yourself.

You want an exercise on how to delete what you don't need? Work with this: Everyone has this one muscle that's essential to focusing, prioritizing, and ultimately winning. You can't see it, you can't show it off under your clothes. It's internal: the IDGAF muscle. The medically correct term is the I Don't Give a Fuck muscle. It's stronger in some people than in others, and it gets stronger the more you use it. This is the muscle you flex when you need to make critical decisions about your life and your priorities, when others are telling you what to do, judging your decisions, and distracting you from your mission. You can also use it on yourself, when your fears and doubts are whispering—or screaming—that you're not good enough and you don't know what you're doing.

I hear you. Flex. *And I don't give a fuck.*

But you can't just *say* it, you have to take real action based on a real decision.

The first few times you use your IDGAF muscle, it may feel weak and sore and easily fatigued, as with any muscle you don't use often enough. But when you use it regularly, and train it appropriately, it becomes strong, fast, and responsive. And that elevates your ability to separate from the things and people you need to move away from.

This muscle should never be used in anger, or to make an emotional decision. This is about making a decision you've wanted to make for a long time, a decision you knew was right but for whatever reason you didn't take action.

You can use this muscle in almost every area of your life, but it's an especially powerful tool in the area of balance. This is the muscle that gives you freedom. *I won't be at this event. I have another commitment. That doesn't work for me. Not doing it.*

The IDGAF muscle is the power behind the Delete button.

Stop spending time you don't have, on people you don't like, doing things you don't want to do. What *do* you want? More time to work? More focus on your goals? More time in your relationship? More time to yourself? Figure it out and make a decision, otherwise you won't be happy in anything.

And when you do make that decision, stop apologizing for it. If you need to acknowledge the difficulty of the choice you made, do it . . . *once.* After that, every apology you make weakens your confidence and belief that you made the right choice. If you truly DGAF, then don't.

I know there are those who can't buy into this. "Oh, if only it was that easy . . ." It *is* that easy, when you know what you want and what you don't want. If you want to win, if you want success, I mean really *want* it—not just kinda sorta want it if things work out—you'll know for sure what you do not GAF about, and what to delete.

That's how you create balance that leads to success.

Picture a scale. On one side you have Winning. That's it. All your dreams and goals and ambitions—they all go on that one side. On the other side, everything else. Family, friends, entertainment, vacations, commitments, obligations . . . whatever else is in your life.

If you're reading this book, I'll assume the Winning side of the scale probably carries more weight than the other side.

But maybe you feel you need more balance, so you start messing with that scale, adding and subtracting from both sides. Work a little less, visit your in-laws more . . . stop checking emails on weekends, start hanging out with your friends . . . invest less money on your business, spend more on the new car. Keep tinkering with that combination, until you finally achieve perfect balance. Everything is even and equal. Congratulations.

Now look at the result. What's the number on a perfectly balanced scale?

Zero.

You want zero happiness?

You want zero success?

You want zero results?

You want zero achievement?

You gave everything equal weight, and balanced yourself right out of the race.

If you want to excel at anything, you can't live in a state of total balance. Winning needs to dominate that scale until its side dips as low as it can go, under the weight of your commitment. It can't completely collapse under the weight, like a seesaw when one kid jumps off too fast and the other side comes crashing down, but it has to withstand as much as you can take. Maybe a little more.

It's your responsibility to remain in charge of that scale, so you're controlling it and it's not controlling you. When it gets too heavy, when you need to add a little more to the other side to lift you back up, you decide what's being added. No one else gets to decide that for you.

Now you're starting to create balance for yourself.

Stop depriving yourself of what you need to perform at the highest level. You need to be able to focus. You need sleep. You need to eat well. You need to stay healthy. Stop feeling guilty about taking care of yourself. It's essential if you're going to go the distance, and it's the best way to take care of everyone else who's relying on you.

Believe me, I understand the conflict. No one wants to lose a relationship or hurt the family or damage friendships. But, guaranteed, if you're chasing a dream or working tirelessly toward a goal, it's costing you something in your personal life. And if it isn't, you're probably not fully committed to those dreams and goals.

That's for you to decide. But I don't know too many

high-achievers who haven't struggled with relationships. I don't care what they show on their social media or the family holiday card. I know too many "successful" people who constantly flaunt a perfectly balanced family life, when the complete opposite is true. Those who brag about balance the most usually have the least. It's a show, driven by guilt and regret. Don't fall for it. Believe what you know, not what you're allowed to see.

At some point there's going to be a disconnect between the pursuit of Winning, and giving energy to everything else around you. Others will say "You're a million miles away." You'll think to yourself: *Only a million?* And then you'll realize: You're exactly where you need to be.

I watch my clients go through this every day, every season, every year. They miss birthdays. Holidays. Mother's Day. Father's Day. Graduations. Weddings. Christmas. If you're an NBA superstar, you're rarely home for Christmas.

Most people shrug and say, "They get paid plenty to do that." Yes, they do. Doesn't make it any easier when you're not there to play Santa for your kids or watch them open presents, or when you're missing the birth of your child because you're in another city competing for a championship.

Living without balance means asking others in your life to understand, support, and wait. It takes a strong and confident person to stand with you while you chase your dreams, and put everything else in your life on hold. Someone who believes in you and what you're doing, and understands that a win for you is a win for everyone in your circle.

It takes someone as fucked up as you are.

Great partners share your obsession and commitment. They don't think you're crazy, they *know* you're crazy, and that's what they love about you. You tell them your plans, and even if they don't completely understand where you're headed, they know *you* know exactly where you're headed. They only question they'll ask is: *You want me to drive?*

If you can find that person, consider yourself fortunate. Your greatest partnerships, relationships, marriages, friendships, will be with people who share your craziness for the end result. That's why I work so well with my clients. I'm as obsessed and fucked up as they are about Winning.

If you need partnership and support, ask for it, don't just assume you're entitled to it, and keep those people alongside you, not behind you in the background. If they're important to you, let them be important. They can't feel as if it's all about you, and they're stuck in *your* dreams with nothing for themselves. They have their own dreams, and if you're not willing to support their aspirations, they probably won't stick around to support yours. Everyone has a responsibility to keep creating wins that benefit the partnership. Your respective ambitions don't have to intersect, you don't have to love what the other is doing. It doesn't mean working in the same business or even doing the same job. It means being aligned with what each of you needs to do, with total mutual respect and support. Without that, it's a broken partnership.

Your partner's role is as important as yours, and if you want to keep him or her happy in that role, you need to be realistic about what's ahead. If you say you need a month to handle your business, handle it in a month. If you need five years, admit it's going to take five years. Don't ask for "a couple of months" and then still be absent—physically and/or mentally—ten years later.

Be honest: *This is going to be hard. It might not be pleasant. I'm doing this for us, and I appreciate what it will cost you. Stick with me. It will be worth it.*

Then make sure it's actually worth it.

When you're present, *be* present. Put the phone down. Close the laptop. Don't just "carve out time" for the people in your life, invest in that time. Give something back to those who have given to you. Your race isn't over, and you still need them. Make it worth their time to continue investing in that.

Balance is an unforgiving tug-of-war, with Winning on the other side. The flag is in the middle, right where balance lives. It's not here or there, it's not winning or losing. Dead center. Average. If you compete hard enough, you can pull Winning over to your side. If you lose, Winning drags you into the mud. Your objective is to fight like hell with everything you have, capture Winning, and win the war.

Ready?

You manage to pull Winning a little closer to you, and as soon as that flag moves off-center, balance weakens. Good start, but you're not there yet. You dig in deeper, and realize you're being pulled in the other direction, not by Winning but by other obligations. Gotta cut them loose. Now you can pull harder, with more determination. You want this so badly, but you're distracted by other things and realize that for now, you have to block out everything but this competition. Total focus. Balance is completely gone, and now your focus gets sharper, your anger gets stronger, your muscles are burning, the skin is tearing off your hands. You can't breathe. More. Harder. Another step, pulling until your arms are trembling. It's just you and Winning now. One more step . . . almost there . . . and Winning takes a giant leap backward, laughing, and yanks you back to where you started.

Flag back to the middle. Balance restored.

Yet you can't let go. You cannot let go. You can't lose. You've come so far and sacrificed so much.

You don't even realize how filthy you are. You're oblivious to the mud on your shoes, the bleeding blisters on your hands—you simply don't care and you won't stop until you win or Winning makes you quit. And you're not going to quit.

Then you look around and realize: No baggage. No distractions. It was just you, fighting for yourself and everyone you care about. Fighting for everything.

For that time, you're not thinking about anything else. You're 100 percent invested in what you're doing, and everything else can wait.

There is no balance here.

You pick up that rope again. You get a towel and wipe the blood off your hands, and make sure Winning sees it; that's its aphrodisiac. And then you keep going. The tug-of-war with Winning continues.

Or, you can stay in the middle, perfectly balanced, and walk away. Back to safety, back to neutral. Not here or there, not forward or back, not up or down. You're not alone anymore, because everyone else is in the middle with you, where no decisions or commitments are made, and you can stay average forever. It's nice. It's calm. But it sure as hell ain't Winning.

This is your battle, your race to greatness. How you achieve it, and whether you achieve it, relies solely on your "selfish" ability to prioritize without regret.

#1.
WINNING IS SELFISH

At the start of the Bulls' Last Dance season, Scottie Pippen announced he'd be having ankle surgery to repair a ruptured tendon. Scottie was my client at the time, and we'd discussed whether he should have the surgery during the summer before that '97–'98 season, so he could be ready to play when the season opened.

But Scottie opted to wait, in part because he didn't want to deal with it over the summer, and also because he was unhappy with his contract, which made him the 6th-highest player on the Bulls and 122nd-highest paid in the league that season. Against the advice of his own agents as well as Bulls owner Jerry Reinsdorf, Scottie had agreed to a contract extension that was well below his value, because he wanted the security of a long-term deal. And now he was unhappy about it.

He figured they weren't paying him enough to rush back.

If you watched *The Last Dance*, you may recall that the team had already been told '97–'98 would be the end of their run. Coach Phil Jackson wouldn't be asked to return, essentially because of a rift between him and GM

Jerry Krause, and because some of the players, including Scottie, wouldn't be re-signed. So the Bulls' second greatest player decided to have the surgery at the start of the season, and missed the first thirty-five games.

In one of the more controversial moments of *The Last Dance*, Michael referred to teammate Scottie Pippen as "selfish."

"Scottie was wrong in that scenario," Jordan said. "He could've got his surgery done as soon as the [previous] season was over and been ready for the [next] season. What Scottie was trying to do was try to force management to change his contract. Jerry wasn't going to do that. So now I got to start the season knowing that Scottie wasn't going to be around.

"I felt like Scottie was being selfish, worrying about himself as opposed to what his word was to the organization as well as to the team."

But not all of their teammates felt that way.

"Everyone respected Scottie so much," said Steve Kerr. "We felt his frustration. He probably should have been the second-highest-paid guy in the NBA. So we all felt for him, nobody resented him for having that surgery. We all understood, let's give him his space, and he's going to be there for the second stretch of the season for us."

The fallout from that episode was immediate. Some felt Scottie had been selfish for putting his needs ahead of the team. But many felt Michael was selfish for blasting a teammate who'd been by his side all the way and whom he had called "the greatest teammate I ever had."

You tell me: Selfish? Both? Neither?

I don't want you to answer yet. Read a little further and we'll come back to it.

Start here: What's your definition of "selfish"?

I'll give you a few options, and you can add your own: Egocentric. Narcissistic. Self-centered. Self-absorbed. Vain. Conceited.

Asshole.

If you've been called any (or all) of those things—which is likely if you're working on the balance issue we just discussed—it probably wasn't meant as a compliment and you were probably offended.

Winning would like you to just say "thank you" and keep on doing whatever you were doing.

The fact is: Winning requires selfishness. Winners don't care what you think. They know how to say no and feel good about it. They have no problem ending a business meeting after ninety seconds because they've heard enough. They don't pretend to like an idea just to make others feel good. They never commit to anything unless they see a benefit to themselves or their goals. Their time and agenda is their top priority, and they don't reach out to others unless they need to. Which they rarely do.

Selfish? Probably. Effective? They let their results speak for themselves.

Winners don't need to be liked. They just need those results, and if they achieve them they don't regret being what you consider "selfish."

Which leads me back to Scottie. Did I agree with his decision? I would have preferred he'd been ready to start the season with the rest of the team. But he did what he felt was right for himself, he knew the ramifications of his actions, he knew MJ would be unhappy with him, and he was willing to accept that. Selfishness requires you to stand by your choices, and be courageous about the backlash.

And when he returned to the team, we made sure he was ready to play. He faced his teammates, and they all got back to work. He started every game for the rest of the season, averaging 37.5 minutes and 19.1 points per game. End result: the sixth ring.

As for MJ, there was no way he was going to pretend to be fine with Scottie's decision. If Michael thinks you're wrong, he has no problem holding you accountable. But he knew what ultimately mattered, and he never failed to credit Scottie with much of his own success. The first person he mentioned in his Hall of Fame speech? "You never just saw me," he said. "You saw Scottie Pippen."

Scottie knew he'd be judged for his decision. MJ knew he'd be judged for his response.

Neither one cared.

When *The Last Dance* was released, and people got to see the true nature of MJ's relationships with teammates and other players around the league (such as in his comments about Scottie), many were quick to point out how harsh and abusive he could be, sometimes good-naturedly, sometimes not. Of course, many of the players pointing out the harshness had been on the receiving end. But many others were critical of the way MJ pressured those who didn't play up to his standards, and how he made it clear there was only one way to play with him—*his* way. The way that had earned six championships.

Results matter.

You might be reading this and thinking, *That's just not me.* Maybe not. But I'd be willing to wager if you really look deeper, you'll see the things you do for yourself, maybe without even thinking about it, that others might consider selfish. It's in *all* of us. When you truly want the end result, those things are no longer a choice. They're a necessity.

I know many psychologists and "experts" talk about the positive benefits of being supportive and positive and tolerant, as opposed to being tough, strict, harsh, or critical. If that softer approach has worked for you—I mean with measurable results, not just as something that makes you the "popular" team leader—then keep doing what you're doing.

Michael knew one way, and it worked. Not just for himself, but for everyone else around him.

If that made him selfish, he'd gladly show you his six rings and say, "You're welcome."

Why is it so wrong to be considered "selfish"?

The word "self" literally relates to your identity, your individuality. Self defines who you are. There are books, songs, T-shirts, posters, and four billion Facebook posts telling you to "Love yourself!" "Find yourself!" "Take care of yourself! "Be yourself!"

If you're going all-in on your *self* . . . wouldn't that make you selfish?

Like that's a bad thing?

It's *not* a bad thing. And it's essential if you're going to win.

Now, let's be clear on one thing before you make a huge mistake: There's a difference between selfish winners and selfish losers. A selfish loser takes from everyone, doesn't know how to use what he's taken, and no one benefits, including the loser. Example: a player who becomes a distraction to the team, plays badly, and blames everyone else. Example: a business owner who pays himself well but neglects the business, pays his employees less than their value so they have no incentive to produce, blames the employees for weak performance, and the business fails. Example: parents who blow off their kids' events, because they're tired, bored, or just don't want to be bothered.

We're not going for that kind of selfish.

We're talking about the ability to focus on your *self*, for all the right reasons. Selfish winners give to themselves, so they can ultimately give to others. They give themselves confidence. Courage. Clarity. They give themselves time and space and focus; they give themselves the freedom to win. They know when to put themselves first, and they don't feel bad about that, because their success fuels everyone around them. Some of the most charitable people in the world—Warren Buffett, Bill and Melinda Gates, the Walton family—are able to give billions to the causes they support because of decades of selfish hard work and commitment.

Tiger Woods's entire upbringing was centered around his parents' total—and some would say selfish—focus on Tiger's career. Earl and Kultida Woods created a lifestyle for themselves and their son that allowed the family to be completely and selfishly devoted to his golf and academic education and massive success. They gave everything they had for him, because they believed in the outcome. He was their one and only priority.

Why is it so difficult to prioritize yourself? And why do others get so agitated when you do? When you're doing the things everyone approves of—eating, sleeping, exercising, socializing, meditating—no one would call you selfish. They can relate to those things because they're, you know, *normal*. But start doing things no one else is doing, things they don't approve of or understand, and you're going to hear about it.

So we come up with cute ways to "normalize" our need to put ourselves first. The "bucket list." The "man cave." "Me time." "Girls' Night Out." Anything to avoid calling it what it really is: time and space that is all about you.

I'm talking to everyone who says "I have no time for myself." Yes, you do. You've just chosen to spend it on something else. You can't get to the gym, you can't start that new project, you can't take your career to the next level, you can't spend a day doing absolutely nothing . . . why? *I have no time for myself. I have too much to do. I made a promise to someone. I can't say no.*

Fact: You can't help all of those other people until you can first help yourself.

You must get comfortable with that. You can't create your own wins without prioritizing your own goals and dreams. It's not selfish to use that "NO List" and the IDGAF muscle we talked about in our discussion on balance. It's crucial to your success.

Selfishness allows you to limit who gets into your inner circle. When you're prioritizing your time and energy, you're going to have to make tough choices about who to include in those priorities. Your family? Your friends? People who want to tell you what's best for you? People who tell you what you want to hear? If you're surrounded by others who keep reminding you they never see you, you're too busy, you need to relax—it's probably because you have too many friends and not enough allies. Allies understand what you need and what you're fighting for, and you know without a doubt they'll fight with you. Friends sometimes feel threatened by your success. Allies understand that your success doesn't detract from theirs.

But selfishness comes with serious responsibility. If you're going to put yourself first, there has to be an outcome and result that makes it all worthwhile. Did you win? Did your selfishness allow you to create something positive? Did it move you further along to where you need to be? Did it benefit you in a way that made you feel good about your decision, even if no one else agreed with you? Are you willing to pay the price for that?

Part of that price—perhaps the most significant part—is embracing the reality that you'll often make decisions and take actions that will make other people unhappy.

And eventually, you'll learn not to care.

That's how you distance yourself from everything and everyone who stands between you and Winning: You learn to separate.

But separation isn't just about moving away from others. It's about moving away from yourself, changing your own limiting beliefs and habits, your own insecurities and fears, and creating new expectations and values. It's about putting new demands on yourself, and shutting out the noise that wants to prevent you from acting on them.

Separation is about creating new levels in everything you do, from your philosophies and strategies to your mental approach to excellence. You don't need to be as good as everyone else. You need to be better.

Separation is power. Power over your decisions, power to move from where you are to where you want to be. Power to stop living a story that someone else has written for you.

Power to elevate yourself.

Separation is also freedom. When you've earned the ability to move away from average and typical and "normal," you've also earned the right to laugh when someone tells you to "stay in your lane." You have no lane. The whole road is open, and it all belongs to you. You're free to decide, act, choose.

Separation is all about you, and what you really want and need. It's that moment before you do something new and bold and terrifying, when it would be so easy to go back to safety, but you know what that safety will cost you. So you take the leap, knowing you can't stay where you are any longer.

It's not easy, and it won't be guilt-free. If you've ever had to break away from your family or friends, if you've left your team to join another team, if you've ever gone against tradition or custom, you already know this. Others won't like it, and they'll let you know. You'll have to brace yourself for the storm that goes along with disappointing people who feel they should have a voice in all your decisions; you'll have to decide whether you need the outcome more than you need their approval.

So when they say "Are you crazy?" you must be prepared to say "Yes. Yes I am. Thank you." Because if you're committed to winning, if you're determined to achieve greatness, you gotta have some crazy in you. You need to have a vision and dream that others can't even comprehend, and you have to be okay with that. Your results will explain everything. I know mine did.

I'm the youngest son of Indian parents who brought our family to the United States when I was four. Both of my parents worked in the medical field, and I was raised to understand that I had two choices for a career: I could be a doctor, or I could be a doctor. I chose neither. I wanted to work with professional athletes.

"You're going to *what*??" My parents grieved. "I'm going to work with professional athletes." But to make them happy—because I genuinely wanted to make them happy, I just didn't want to be a doctor—I agreed to apply to medical school, and I prayed I wouldn't get in.

I got in. Which led to one of the most difficult "selfish" moments of my life: telling my parents I wasn't going to medical school, and wasn't going to be a doctor.

To say that they were disappointed would be a wild understatement, even though I went on to get my master's degree in exercise science, and managed to have a decent career doing exactly what I said I would do: work with professional athletes. But I was blessed with parents who loved and supported me even though they disagreed with my decision (although even after all my success with MJ and Kobe and Wade and others, they'd still casually mention the upside of a "real job" with benefits and a 401[k]).

Was I selfish? I'll let you decide. I made a choice for myself, separated from my family's expectations, and devoted my life to the results. I hope you have the opportunity to be just as selfish someday.

Most of what I've done in my career has been about separation. When I started training MJ in 1989, it was rare for trainers to work directly with pro athletes; trainers typically worked for the teams, which is how they got access to the players. But MJ wanted separation from the Bulls' standard training procedures, which was why he hired me; he wanted a program developed for his unique needs. So when the team tried to tell me how to train him, I was polite but kept my distance. And I realized that to be effective for my client, and all the clients who'd follow, I'd need to remain that way.

To this day, I've never been employed by a team. I consult for teams, I collaborate with teams, but my work has always been for the individual athlete. I need that defined separation to do my job effectively.

But separation doesn't mean you cut all ties and refuse to cooperate. Collaboration and cooperation are essential in my business, and probably in yours too. I've worked with many corporate groups who struggle with a "Fuck those guys" attitude within the business, where different teams and departments wage war on each other's procedures and results. Some believe it creates a healthy competitive environment and a "badass" mentality that drives people to raise the bar on their performance. But if you've ever worked in such a culture, you know it rarely turns out that way.

For me to be effective in my business, I need to know that everyone involved with my client is on the same page, and they need to know that as well. That means respectful communication with team personnel, from the president and GM to the training staff and other professionals involved in our shared outcome. You need him to come in at this weight? You want to address these issues in his game? How do you plan to use him this season? I got it. We'll keep in touch. I'm always open and cooperative, which has earned me tremendous trust from teams who are customarily wary of "outsiders."

I also separate when it comes to talking about my clients' progress and workouts. I rarely post video or pictures of my work with athletes, and I rarely talk about what we're doing. I know it's standard now for trainers to use social media to show off their clients, not only in the gym but in the clubs, on the golf courses, at the pool, on vacation. I go the other way. Here's the extent of my social media as it relates to my athletes: If you're relevant to my client—immediate family, agent, team personnel, health professional—*and* you have his or her permission, I'm happy to send you video and pictures. You have full access to whatever we're doing. Or if my clients want to post our work in their social media, or they ask me to post something, that's up to them. Otherwise I need to keep our work separate from the entertainment and media aspect of the business, and protect my clients from people who don't need to be in their business.

One of the reasons I'm hired to work with corporate leaders and business owners and celebrities is because I value privacy and discretion. I won't talk to the media about what we're doing, I'm not going to screenshot their texts to post on social media, I don't walk into meetings with a camera crew following me around.

Why does any of this matter? Because Winning insists on being your sole priority. And that requires your full attention, your total focus, and the unlimited ability to invest in your results. To me, posting your workouts on social media isn't the kind of investment that delivers results. It gets attention, but not results. And if I do my job, if my clients do theirs, the end results speak for themselves, other people can talk about them, and we never have to post a thing.

Winning is an investment. It's the result of making "selfish" choices that empower your goals, separate you from limitations and insecurities, and create distance between where you've been and where you want to go.

Those things don't happen accidentally. They happen when you make the decision to prioritize your ambitions and your results. It's the single greatest investment you can make in your life, and until you're ready to commit to that, you can't even think about Winning.

If you know you should be getting better results, and

you believe you're worth the commitment to get those results, it's time to be selfish and invest. For some, that means allocating financial resources. For others, it's about education and learning. It might be a decision to change jobs or lose weight or quit smoking or work on a relationship. It can mean time or money or a shift in the way you think. That's for you to determine. But whatever that investment requires, make it, because no one is going to make it for you.

How can you expect others to believe in you when you won't believe in yourself?

People hesitate to invest in themselves for so many reasons. It feels egotistical. They think they're not worth it. They believe they'll fail. They think others will judge them. Maybe it's a waste of money. "Can I afford to do this?" they wonder. My question to them: Can you afford *not* to?

If you own a successful business that requires constant travel to multiple locations, is it really a "luxury" to invest in a corporate jet so you can use your time and resources more effectively? Or if you can't afford the jet, is it "wasteful" to join an airport lounge or fly first class, so you have some room to work while you travel? If your business involves driving colleagues to look at potential real estate investments, is it "flashy" to invest in a nice car so your passengers are comfortable? If you're working remotely and conducting all your meetings and conferences online, shouldn't you consider spending some money on quality equipment that allows you to look and sound professional?

I'm always amazed when the media report on superstar athletes who spend hundreds of thousands of dollars—or more—on their training and health, as if that's a crazy luxury. *There's a chef! And a masseuse! He's got a whole gym and a basketball court in the house!* Those aren't luxuries, those are business partners. You're talking about athletes with eight- or nine-figure incomes. You don't think they should invest 1 percent of that to make sure they're strong and healthy? To prolong their careers so they can keep making the kind of money that allows them to spend that kind of money?

But let's be clear on this: It's not about how much money is being spent. The financial investment is worthless if you're not also investing your time and effort in the end result. How many times have you walked away from the opportunity to get better in some way? When you knew what you had to do, but didn't do it? How often have you tried "reinventing" yourself, instead of investing in who you already are?

I hear from so many young people who want to get into the training business and work with the pros. They want to know how to make that happen, like there's a secret code that will give them access. I have only one answer, regardless of whether you want to work with athletes or design skyscrapers or discover a planet: invest in your education and your skills. There are no shortcuts, there's no fast track. Michael Jordan hired me because I presented him with a program that intrigued him, and then I backed it up with results. The years I spent investing in myself—learning, experimenting, developing a plan that would someday change the way athletes trained—allowed that to happen.

It's up to you to make that happen for yourself. If your family isn't supportive, if they think you're going to fail, if they're telling you it's too hard and too much and you're making the biggest mistake of your life, you can either agree and live the life they've chosen for you, or you can take responsibility for yourself and find a way to live the life you want.

You already know what I'd do.

I know there are many highly successful people who didn't go to college and strongly believe *you* don't need college either. They'll tell you it's a waste of money, you can be successful without it, they did it and so can you. I strongly disagree. It worked for them, that's great. But what about all the *unsuccessful* people who didn't go to college? Are you positive opting out of that experience will still allow you to achieve everything you want, now and in the future? What's the downside to getting the education, challenging yourself to finish something? You don't have to go to a big four-year institution, but get something that separates you from others, that shows you've elevated beyond the pack.

Winning requires a combination of street education, formal education, common sense—which is not always that common—and uncommon sense, because Winning is definitely uncommon.

They can take everything from you—your house, money, clothes, cars, jets. But the one thing they can't take is your education and what you've learned. And the one thing you can count on if you do indeed lose everything is that education.

Invest in yourself because you're worth it. It's not selfish to want more; it's necessary to survive the hell of Winning.

#1.

WINNING TAKES YOU TO HELL. AND IF YOU QUIT, THAT'S WHERE YOU'LL STAY

Late one night in 2007, Kobe Bryant called Michael Jordan for advice. His knees were killing him, he said. He'd already played ten seasons in the league, and believed he could play ten more, but he wasn't sure how much longer he could withstand the physical toll. He didn't know how much more those knees could give him.

MJ understood. "Call Grover," he said. "He'll take care of you." He was already retired, and after fifteen years with me, he was more than happy to see me showing up at someone else's door at 5:00 a.m.

He shared with Kobe some of what we'd done together, and why he thought I was the answer Kobe was looking for. "He's the biggest asshole you'll ever meet," said MJ, "but he knows his stuff."

You really cannot ask for a better compliment from Michael Jordan.

Kobe had already won championships in 2000, 2001,

and 2002, and was already established as one of the best to ever play the game. But the team had fallen from dynasty to disaster: Shaquille O'Neal was unhappy and demanding a trade, which ultimately sent him to Miami. Coach Phil Jackson left just ahead of being fired, and wrote a book that was highly critical of Kobe. The team became mired in a long, painful rebuilding. And now Kobe was faced with the very real and uncomfortable possibility that three rings would be it for him.

By 2007, it had been five years since the last championship, and Winning was no longer taking Kobe's calls.

He could have quit, taken his three rings, and said "good enough." He could have given in to his deteriorating knees, played less, and slowly wound down the clock on his career.

Instead, he called me.

I cherish being the last call someone makes when nothing else is working. That's Winning to me.

The first time I put him through a workout, he looked at me after an hour, dripping with sweat, and asked: "What we got left?"

I told him: The road to paradise starts in hell.

Kobe had been to paradise, and he'd lived through hell. And he had no problem going back and forth between the two.

Our work together wasn't easy, and he didn't ask for it to be easy. We had to change his body without changing his game, and he understood that everything we did would be new and different for him, from his exercises and training regimen to his sleep schedule and diet. Everyone who worked with him, from the team staff to other elite practitioners, all knew the challenge: We were going to a new level.

Winning only gives you another win if you fight for it, with greater obsession than you fought for it the first time.

The work we did definitely qualified as hell. Not because it was brutally long or unnecessarily punishing—I don't believe in that—but because we had a serious goal that required serious detail. Other teammates and players in the off-season saw what we were doing and asked to join. They never came back a second time.

For example: I'd have him hold a deep lunge position, with his back leg as straight as possible and the knee as close to the ground as possible without touching it, while practicing perfect shooting form with a basketball . . . for five minutes. On each leg.

Try it. You'll hear Winning laughing somewhere in the distance.

Sometimes, I would make a space sixteen feet wide, fifteen feet long, and mark off an area that replicated the NBA paint. Our workouts were done in that small space. I'd have him pivot, turn, jump, stop, go, in every direction and at every speed, with and without a ball. Then I'd ask him what movements made him feel pain. I needed to know if he felt discomfort right away, after two or three steps, when he stopped, started, jumped, or landed . . . every detail. We'd identify it, address it, and work to make that area pain-free. Then we'd move on to another movement, and work to make that pain-free as well. And so on and so on, every day. He never hesitated, never skipped a workout, never backed away from a difficult challenge.

When people talk of Kobe's greatness, they often say, "He put in the work." True, but they're missing the point. Players like MJ and Kobe didn't just work, they constantly and consistently *elevated* the work, because to get out of hell, you have to elevate *everything*. They never stayed with what got them there, they were always adding pieces that would take them higher. They understood that if you keep doing the same thing, you're going to get the same results. So to get better, they had to put in *new* work, *different* work.

If you don't evolve, if you don't find new ways to challenge yourself, you're a BlackBerry in a world of iPhones. Everyone else keeps improving, and you're still running the old tired software.

Kobe and I shared the same obsessions: prolonging his career, bringing him back to full strength—not just as good as he was but better than ever—and of course, Winning.

By 2009, Kobe had his next win. And another in 2010.

A reporter asked him during the 2009 Finals how he was feeling. "I feel great," he said. "This is the best I've felt this late in the season my whole career."

A win for me, to see him healthy, strong, and back in Winning's elite club. Welcome back to paradise.

But the road to paradise is a two-way street, and just as quickly as you travel to the top, you can slide right back down. In fact, you can pretty much count on it. Winning doesn't let you hang around. It meets you at the parade, cheers the loudest when you get the trophy, and then escorts you out to the parking lot, where the bus that brought you has a new sign with its next destination: "Hell."

It would be ten years before the Lakers returned to the Finals again.

People think of Winning as this gorgeous magnificent triumph that solves everything. And it does . . . for a moment. But stay in that moment too long, and Winning will make sure you never have that moment again.

It's a never-ending cycle, not a one-way trip. You want to win? Start at the bottom and work your way up. Congrats, you won. You want to feel that way again? Go back to the bottom and work your way up. Congrats, you won. You want to feel that way again? Go back to the bottom and . . . right. You get it.

And even when you get to the top, Winning expects you to carry a piece of hell with you, so you never forget where you came from—and never forget you can be sent back there at any moment.

Winning is a painkiller for the side effects of hell. The crushing mental and physical pressure, the ruined relationships, the judgmental friends, the long hours, the relentless work—they can all be alleviated by success. Everything you want for yourself—satisfaction, pride, money, fame, glory, security—can all be yours with a powerful and sustained dose of Winning.

But here's the message on the warning label: Winning is a drug that requires a more powerful dose every time you take it. With every win, you learn more, you experience more, you know what can go wrong and you know how you have to prepare for the return trip to the top. So that dosage has to steadily become more potent to work. You can't just take it in small amounts: you have to be addicted.

MJ understood this better than most, as well as the essential return to hell; it's one of the things that made him great. Early in his career, he knew the hell of being physically beaten on the court by the Detroit Pistons. He knew the hell of building up his body until he was so strong he no longer had to take the abuse. He was in the league seven seasons—yes, seven—before finally getting to paradise, for the first of his six dances with Winning.

Then: back to hell. His father was murdered, the media and public scrutiny of Michael's life were out of control, and in 1993 he decided to walk away from the NBA to chase another dream: He wanted to play baseball. For two seasons, he played in 127 minor-league games, rode minor-league buses, and was working his way up to the majors when MLB players went on strike in 1994–95. He was asked to cross the picket line and continue playing; he refused and decided it was time to go back to his first love: basketball. He wanted to win again.

When he returned to the NBA mid-season in 1995, we had two months to get him ready for the playoffs. Baseball had conditioned his body to move and perform in an entirely different way, and we had a relatively short period of time to reestablish his basketball body. It wasn't enough. The Bulls lost to the Orlando Magic in the 1995 playoffs, and many believed that the "real" MJ was done. "You can't take off two years and return the same way," they said. "It's over."

Show me, said Winning.

Watch me, said MJ.

On the night the Bulls lost to the Magic, we sat in the darkened arena after everyone had left. There wasn't a lot to say, but the silence said it all, and when he was finally ready to go, I figured it was the last time I'd see him for a while; he usually took time off at the end of the season before we started training again.

"Call me when you're ready," I said. "Let me know when you want me to see you."

"I'm ready," he answered. "I'll see you tomorrow."

Time to get out of hell.

It was a trip he'd made so many times, at the start of every season. He understood nothing was promised; there were no guarantees he'd be as good or better than the season before. Everything he did, all the success—he worked for it and earned it.

So as one season ended and the next approached, he knew what to expect and what to demand of himself. He didn't fear the annual hell that awaited, because every trip back made him tougher, stronger, more resilient. That was his power.

Your first trip to hell is terrifying. By the second or third visit, you know what to expect, what has to be done. Resilience isn't built in your comfort zone; it's built in hell. And every time you go back you're a little harder, rougher, less emotional, more scarred. After you've made the journey repeatedly for years and decades, you barely feel the heat.

But his teammates did, as they faced an even fiercer MJ when they all returned the following season, for the start of another run at greatness that began with the legendary 72–10 season and ended with three more rings. Everyone would come in to practice happy and relaxed... until hell walked through that door, disguised as Michael Jordan.

Demanding, intimidating, cruel, driven beyond measure. And if you had a problem with that, as he said in *The Last Dance*, "you never won anything." His teammates will tell you, without hesitation, that he was indeed hell to play with. But he took every one of them to paradise.

Athletes and celebrities—even some CEOs and business moguls—experience the journey in public. Most people don't; that endless ride between paradise and hell happens in private, where no one knows or understands what you're dealing with.

Everyone is going through something you know nothing about. Pressure, fear, mental and physical pain, self-doubt, sacrifice, the grind that never stops. It's the business owner who has to lay off half her staff just to keep the company afloat. The parents who aren't sure they can cover the bills. It's the uncertainty about whether you made the right career choice, or whether your relationship is worth keeping. It's looking at yourself in the mirror, and wondering if you'll ever be enough.

For some it's working for a horrible boss, dealing with health issues, dealing with difficult family issues. I don't think there's a lonelier experience than looking for answers, finding none, and realizing you're at the crossroads of your life: Either you fight your way out of the hell you're in, or start accepting that you'll be there forever.

Your business can have its best month ever, and on the first of the next month, you're back to zero, back to do it all over again, this time with higher expectations. And if you're the leader of that business, you have to get the entire team to keep taking that trip with you as well, and not exhale along the way.

Winning waits to see what you'll do. It doesn't care about being fair—doesn't care about your talent or skill or how hard you worked. It just wants you to figure it out and fight for it.

If it makes you feel any better, you'll have a lot more company in hell than you will at the top. Hell is where most people stay, because as unpleasant as it may be, for many it's easier to settle there than try to battle their way out, and everyone there can relate to each other's troubles. Weight, finances, relationships, careers . . . hell is packed with folks who are struggling with the same issues. So many, in fact, that it starts to feel right. Normal. You fit right in.

But you're still in hell, and without a decisive plan to escape, that's where you'll remain.

For some, hell is about the hard work and endless battle to improve. But for others, hell is the chilling realization that they're stuck, and will probably stay that way.

People will tell you to "just push through it," as if there's a one-way door to Winning that swings wide open. Pushing isn't enough, it's unimaginative and predictable. You pushed—and then what? To get out of your own personal hell, you have to be able to pull, grab, reach, climb, slither, jump, dig, claw your way to freedom. Remember MJ's words in *The Last Dance*? "I pulled people along when they didn't want to be pulled." Most people give a little push, and find themselves in a revolving door that just goes around and around and around.

Winning sets unreasonable goals, and requires you to bear the burden of responsibility for achieving them. That means doing anything and everything possible to get out of the situation you're in, and into position to win.

You can pay the price of Winning and succeed, or you can quit, stay where you are, and pay the price of regret.

Winning will use every dirty trick in the book—and make up new ones just to entertain itself—to keep you in hell. *It's too hard*, it whispers . . . *you'll never get there . . . your parents don't believe in you . . . your friends think you're crazy . . . look at you, you're already a failure.* Which, by no coincidence, is exactly what you were already thinking. So you stay there, waiting. Waiting to feel different, waiting to be told what to do, waiting for an answer that never comes. And meanwhile, the flames are getting hotter and hotter, until you can't take it. You have to take action, or you burn out. But instead of being propelled by the heat, you can become frozen where you are.

You have to embrace the negativity, the criticism, the cynicism of others, so you can control how that fire burns. Fire can destroy, but it can also forge new creations. The more you can withstand, and the sooner you take action, the greater your chances of getting back in the race.

For some, it's all too much to deal with—they do nothing and, eventually, Winning gives up on them entirely and moves on. If you don't want more for yourself, that's fine, someone else will get that win. Instead, your hell becomes never knowing what could have been, never having more or doing more for yourself. That's the hell of complacency, the hell of average. It's quiet. There's no rage or fire. Just a silent hell of nothingness.

For others, hell is the result of choices; these people chose a path that looked like Winning, and got everything they wanted, but realized too late they hated the path they chose. That's the player who takes the big contract but ends up on a losing team, the CEO with a successful business who hates what he does, the relationship that fails because you chose the wrong partner. That's the hell of wanting and needing something different.

Often, that's when Winning walks away from you: *I gave you an opportunity, and you blew it.* It may allow you back in through some other endeavor, but not that one. Sorry, we're closed. For now. Back to hell for more time to make the transition.

For many, that kind of disappointment and failure is a hard stop. For the greats, it's the start of a new race.

When Winning took Kobe's Achilles and his dreams of a sixth and seventh ring, he had to go win something else. It wasn't enough to win the Oscar and write bestsellers and create films. He was revolutionizing girls' basketball with his daughter Gianna, teaching her and her teammates how to win the Mamba way. While most kids that age practice for forty-five minutes and then have a snack, Kobe held three-hour practices, with two and a half hours devoted just to defense.

He couldn't stop finding ways to win.

But not all athletes are able to transfer their competitive drive into new things to chase, once their careers reach an expiration date.

I'm not talking about pro athletes who have made millions, and—if they've managed their money—can ride for a while on their investments and their fame. Think about Olympians, who make that endless round-trip from hell to Winning every four years, if they do everything right. They might only get there once.

And then what? The rarest of Olympians—Michael Phelps or Simone Biles, for example—might have a career as a spokesperson or speaker or broadcaster. But if you're an archer or a bobsledder or a pole vaulter? What's next for that athlete? You can be the greatest marksman in the world, and now what? Professional sniper? You've trained since you were ten to be the best in the world, and now you have to be an instructor at the shooting range and you can't even afford the bullets. That's your hell, unless you can find the next win for yourself.

I see it in my business all the time, with trainers who managed to work with one famous player, and thought it would give them a permanent ticket to Winning. A year later, they're selling gym equipment in the mall, wondering what happened.

There are wins everywhere. It's on you to keep finding them.

• • •

Everyone has been through something so difficult or painful or challenging that it changed them forever. We may not know it at the time, but those are the situations that break something inside us, and we can never be rebuilt the same way.

That's not a weakness. It's your greatest strength, and your ticket out of hell.

How do you build muscle? You tear it down and it heals stronger. How do you create a scar? You suffer damage, and it heals stronger. Scar tissue is one of the strongest things your body can manufacture.

How do you get back to paradise after going through hell?

You rebuild yourself into something stronger.

Not the same as you were. Stronger than before.

This isn't about picking up the pieces and putting them back together. Try that sometime, with something you broke. A dish, a toy, a mirror. You take all these broken pieces, and try to put them back together like nothing happened. But something did happen, and you can't undo that kind of damage.

You don't pick up the pieces. The pieces have to pick you up, and they decide how you need to be rebuilt. You won't be the same as you were. You'll be stronger, because those broken pieces are bringing experience and pain and grief, and using all of it for fuel.

Not everyone will like how you've been reassembled. They see someone different. They say you've changed. They're right.

To grow your mind, heart, body, and spirituality, you must first accept all your wounds. Welcome them, embrace them. Now you're resilient as you continue your chase; you can't be hurt because whatever your opponents do to you, you've already felt it.

#1.
WINNING IS A TEST WITH NO CORRECT ANSWERS

In the spring of 2020, I jumped out of a perfectly good airplane. I had a parachute, and a guy strapped to my back who knew what the hell to do, but it was still me up there jumping.

The skydive—my first—was something I allegedly promised my daughter we'd do together. She remembered that promise, I did not, but I took her word for it and we went up there together. I was infinitely more concerned for her than for myself, and she wasn't concerned at all. I didn't know how it would feel, to put complete control in the hands of a pilot and guide I'd never met, and just fall into the sky. I'd be lying if I said I didn't feel some fear.

Before we left the house that morning, I'd already studied the physical mechanics of the jump, how the landing would work, the angle of the descent, the way my feet were supposed to hit the ground running. I'm thinking: *Could I fly the plane if something went wrong up there? And what's my plan if the guy's chute doesn't open? Or if he has a heart attack? Or if he's a Pistons fan?*

I had no problem rolling out of the plane into the open sky; that was in my control. But once we were falling, my first thought was to look around for the nearest body of water, the softest possible place to land if something went wrong. If I'm going to be free-falling without a parachute, I'm not going down screaming without at least attempting another option.

And even though my goggles landed somewhere in a Wisconsin cornfield—they blew off immediately—and the whole thing happened so fast I can't even remember all the details, I do know this:

Yes, I felt fear. But I had no doubt that whatever happened, I'd be fine.

I realize that in the worst-case scenario, that might not have been true; I may be relentless, but I'm not stupid. Yet I never allowed myself to think about it that way, I never doubted the outcome.

When you feel fear, when you can't trust anything else, you must be able to trust yourself.

When someone tells you they never feel nervous, or they have no fears, they're either lying, or their challenges aren't big enough.

Everyone experiences fear. Everyone. I don't care how brave and badass and "fearless" you imagine yourself to be; there's something that strikes fear in your soul and makes your heart pound uncontrollably. Maybe just for a moment, maybe longer. You can't prevent it. Fear is instinctive; we're hardwired for it. Not just in sports or adventuring or intense competition, but in business and classrooms and every part of our lives.

I know I don't have to explain fear, you've experienced it a million times in your life—maybe you're experiencing it right now. But we have to talk about it, because fear can give you direct access to Winning, if you know how to manage it.

People don't like to admit fear, because they think it will make them look weak or insecure or panicked. But insecurity and panic aren't the same as fear. They align more with anxiety, and your doubts about your ability to manage the fear. Fear and doubt aren't the same, and the difference is as distinct as Winning and Losing.

What do you fear? What are you afraid of that's holding you back from what you really want?

I'm sure you realize we're not talking about spiders and tall buildings and clowns. We're talking about the chaotic thoughts churning in your head at 2:00 a.m., when you so badly want to sleep but the noise in your mind won't stop.

Whatever you fear, do you face those challenges with the confidence that you can manage the outcome? Or do you doubt your ability to handle what's coming your way?

Fear versus doubt. Not the same thing.

The greats quiet themselves by thinking about all the preparation they've put in, the confidence that they've done the work and they're ready. My basketball clients played eighty-two regular-season games a year, and they felt nervous before every single one. Before every game, you'd see MJ alone, head down, chewing his gum, having a private conversation with himself. He felt the same nerves you might feel before you're about to face a challenge. But he never doubted that he would perform at his best.

Kobe felt it as well. "I have self-doubt," he said in an interview. "I have insecurity. I have fear of failure. I have nights when I show up at the arena and I'm like, 'My back hurts, my feet hurt, my knees hurt. I don't have it. I just want to chill.' We all have self-doubt. You don't deny it, but you also don't capitulate to it. You embrace it."

You embrace it. You trust yourself to handle whatever you're dealing with, and don't allow your fear to escalate into uncontrollable doubt.

If you ever see me at a game, you'll see no emotion from me. I don't jump up at great plays, I don't hang my head when something goes wrong. But every minute, I feel that familiar fear of what could happen to one of my players. I've seen thousands of games, watched a million minutes of my clients performing at the highest level, and every one of those minutes I'm thinking: *Did he land badly? Is he limping? Was it the exercise we did yesterday? Was it the exercise we didn't do yesterday? Why is he missing that shot? Does he look fatigued? How do we address this tomorrow?*

And there may be absolutely nothing wrong at all, but I never stop anticipating it.

That's my fear, my hell. I can't afford to buy into the "Think positive!" mode of problem-solving. When my clients have an issue, thinking positive isn't going to help. My job is to be prepared for any situation, and if I solve enough issues, if I keep stringing together the right answers, they get to go back to paradise, and for a brief moment, so do I. Only for a moment, though, because my work begins again soon, preparing for what's next.

But returning to paradise doesn't happen by the power

of positive thought. It happens because of dedicated and targeted action.

I see too many trainers who only talk about their clients when they're playing well, and then disappear when there's an issue. They want to take all the credit for the good, and zero accountability for the bad. When someone has a great game, the trainer is all over the media talking about his or her great workouts and training. When the athlete has a bad game or gets hurt, the trainer is nowhere to be found, mainly because he fears being blamed for it, and doubts his ability to fix it.

I can't guarantee my athletes aren't going to get injured, but I can't live in fear of it. So everything I do is to minimize the risk of that happening. There's no way to prevent every injury, but I can take every precaution to protect against it.

That helps me fight the mental urge to doubt myself, to create problems that haven't happened and overthink everything that could go wrong.

Fear shows up on its own. Doubt has to be invited. Fear heightens your awareness; it makes you alert. Doubt is the opposite; it slows you down and paralyzes your thinking.

Fear is about playing to win. Doubt is about playing to not lose.

When you're facing a big meeting or huge presentation or the game of a lifetime, fear is a flashing neon strobe that jolts you into action. Doubt tells you to freeze until the crisis has passed.

Fear is about the threat, whatever you have to face. Doubt is about you.

You might fear what the opposition could do. But if you doubt your ability to beat them, you have no chance.

Fear tells you there's a minute left on the clock, and you need to win now. Doubt tells you there's a minute left on the clock, and you're about to lose.

Fear is pressure. Doubt is panic.

Fear says *I can do this.* Doubt says *I'm fucked.*

Of all the obstacles and challenges you'll face on this race to greatness, none will define you more than how you react when you stand at the crossroads of fear and doubt.

That's Winning: a terrifying leap of belief in yourself. Winning takes you up in the plane and pushes you out the door before you can check once more to see if your parachute is harnessed.

You can prepare yourself, you can plan and organize and map out everything you want to do. But at some point, you have to take that jump into the unknown, let the fear flow through you, and believe with total confidence that you'll succeed.

There are four components of Winning that determine how you'll manage your fears and doubts and make that leap, or if you'll make it at all.

Talent.

Intelligence.

Competitiveness.

Resilience.

It's possible to get a win with just three of these, and I suppose in very rare cases, you might be able to stumble into a win with just one or two, if a thousand other things are going in your favor at the same time.

But to win at the highest level, over and over, in all areas of your life—career, finances, health, family, whatever else you value—you need all four.

Very few people have all four.

Picture a bull's-eye. There's a large ring on the outside, with a slightly smaller ring inside that one, and then an even smaller ring inside that one, and then in the very center, one more little ring.

I call these the Four Rings of Winning. And in the dead center of these rings, there's your target.

In the large outer ring, you have talent. Everyone gets into this ring, because everyone has some degree of talent at something. Being in this group isn't elite or remarkable; it's just a starting point you can build on, because talent is never going to be enough to make you a consistent winner. Even if you're extremely talented, there are still going to be others at your level, or close to it, and if they have other abilities you don't possess, you'll be left behind.

Inside that talent ring is a slightly smaller ring. To get into this ring, you need to bring your talent, and you'll also need intelligence. You don't have to be a genius on all topics, but you need extreme intelligence in whatever you're striving to accomplish. The individuals in this ring know how to develop their talent, and they have a deep understanding of how to use it.

So, for example, an NFL quarterback doesn't need to understand how to perform a heart transplant, but he needs to be extremely smart about how to be an NFL quarterback. However: There are plenty of smart and talented people out there who have never achieved anything, so being in this ring isn't necessarily going to guarantee a win. You're going to need more.

Now we move closer to the center of the target, into the next ring, where the population is even smaller. To get into this ring, you must have talent, intelligence, and the added element of competitiveness, because all the ability and smarts in the world can't help you if you're not able or willing to compete for what you want. If you're in this ring, you understand nothing is going to be handed to you, no matter how good you are, and you're committed to fighting for your end result. This is where a lot of people lose: They talk about competing, they say all the right things and truly believe them. They say they'll "do anything" . . . until it's time to "do anything." When it's time to execute and push themselves to the next level, when it's time to step on their opponent's throat with undeniable results, they start to doubt their ability and they pull back. Great competitors don't pull back.

If you're truly competitive, and you can combine that trait with talent and intelligence, you can be very good.

But you need one more thing to be a true winner.

There's one more ring, the smallest, with the fewest people and the greatest results. This tiny circle has all the other components—talent, intelligence, competitiveness—and adds the one thing that separates champions from everyone else:

Resilience.

Resilience is the power to stay in the fight when your

fear is telling you to run. It's the ability to see everything that can go wrong, and still get control of what can go right. When you've been blindsided by bad news, bad people, or bad fortune—when you have nothing to hold on to—resilience is your lifeline.

Resilience is knowing that when everything goes from bad to worse, and you have every reason to fall apart, you don't.

It allows you to feel the pain and humiliation of loss and conflict and turmoil, and still believe you'll survive.

When your head is exploding under the pressure bearing down on you, when your guts are being torn apart by chaos and crisis, when you want to quit, when everyone wants you to quit, resilience is the dark drug that whispers to you: *Keep going.*

Because you know you can. You must.

When you have nothing to lose, you're free to do anything.

You know that uncomfortable jittery feeling of "butterflies" in the stomach? That's resilience, firing up its engines. Those butterflies are your partners, your allies in facing what's in front of you. They remind you there's a battle about to be fought, and you need to go face it. As I said in *Relentless*, you don't need to make them go away. You need to get them all going in the same direction, and use them for energy.

When you hear bad news, when you're backed into a corner, when you realize things are about to go against you, you have two choices: allow the fear to elevate to panic, or put your resilience to work and keep going.

When the NFL kicker misses a field goal in the Super Bowl, when the figure skater falls in the Olympics, when you forget the most important part of your big presentation, there's nothing anyone can say or do to make that sickening feeling go away. And unless you have the resilience to pull yourself together—fast—you're done. You see it all the time in competition: Something goes bad, and everything else gets worse. It takes a rare competitor to stop the free fall, forget about it in that moment, and continue.

Others can give you a thumbs-up and a cheery "You got this!" but let's be honest: If you need someone else to tell you that, if you don't already feel it, you got nothing. You're so low that your teammates can't reach you, until you reach yourself first.

Winning gives you a permanent knot in your stomach, and laughs as you try to untie it.

But you'd better untie it quickly, because you can't make things better for yourself until you stop making them worse.

Resilience is what separates fear and doubt. It allows you to be on high alert, but still remain in control of your decisions and actions.

Resilient people don't act like victims, they don't feel sorry for themselves. They're not dwelling on what's happening right now, they're looking ahead to see how they can take control and change the outcome. If they don't like the way their story is unfolding, they write their own.

There's not a single day of your life that doesn't require some kind of resilience.

Financial trouble. Family issues. Health challenges.

Relationship problems. Job situations. So many things you never thought you'd be dealing with.

We like to think of Winning as this glamorous, glorious achievement, and for those who get there, it is. But very little of what you go through to attain it is glamorous or glorious. It's the reason champions break down with emotion when they finally hold the trophy; they're not thinking about the ring and the parade, they're remembering the pain and frustration, the fear and sacrifice and loneliness. Everything they endured, all the times they wanted to quit but kept going.

They know the truth: Without the resilience to get through the darkest hours of fear and failure, they never would have made it. And if they want to win again, they have to stay resilient against those things all over again.

If you can't handle failure, you can't handle Winning.

Everyone is going to fail, but everyone is *not* going to win. You might be one of a hundred people applying for a job, but only one person is getting hired. There are thirty-two teams in the NFL, only one is winning the Super Bowl. For everyone else, failure. And you have to be resilient in confronting that failure or you'll never survive long enough to reach success.

People love to brag about how they hate to lose, how they're terrible losers, as if somehow that makes them winners. Guess what, everyone hates to lose. No one sits back and says, *You know what, I prefer losing, it feels great.* But to truly understand Winning, you must also understand its partner, Losing.

Winning and Losing aren't mortal enemies; they need

each other to survive. Without Losing, Winning can't exist, because if someone is going to win, that usually means someone else has to lose. It's a bizarre, twisted partnership.

But while Winning is careful and meticulous and elaborately fussy about who gets in, Losing takes everyone, and has no patience for Winning's drama and pickiness. *Take one already*, says Losing, *the rest are mine*.

Winning makes you an expert on Losing. You don't ever get used to it, but you learn to control your reaction, until you have no reaction at all. You become less emotional about it, because the energy it takes to lose your mind over a loss is energy you need to redirect into Winning. And the more you hang on to that emotion, the harder it will be for you to move past it and the harder you'll make it for everyone else to move past it. You understand it's part of the process. You don't have to like it, but you have to face it. It's a necessary evil, and a reality of competition.

If you lost, if you played poorly, if you totally sucked, just say it. *I played poorly. I had a bad game.* You don't have to give a reason, you don't have to explain. It's already obvious to everyone, so just put it out there and get back to work. Then learn from it, absorb it, take everything you can from it . . . and get rid of it. It's over.

Sometimes after a game, and especially after a loss, Kobe obtained the game film and we'd watch it together, every moment, every frame. Sometimes we'd be in the car headed to a late dinner, and we'd never get there; we'd just sit in the car analyzing what went right and what went wrong. That's how you manage a loss. You tear it apart until it loses its power to happen again.

Losing hurts. You don't have to be taught that, every little kid knows losing hurts. What happens when kids are playing, and one gets the toy, or wins the race, or scores a point? The other kid is crying and hitting the winner over the head with a plastic golf club. Either way, there's going to be a reaction, and it's not a happy one.

Winning is instinctive, at any age.

But right away, the grown-ups intervene and lecture the loser: *It's just a game! Have fun! Be nice! Don't be a sore loser!*

Nice? Winning requires more than "nice." In fact, it doesn't require "nice" at all. And what's the opposite of a sore loser? A good loser? What's next, a great loser?

I'm not going to tell anyone how to raise their kids. But let's be honest: You don't like to lose either. The way you manage Losing says everything about how you'll manage Winning. The lesson isn't "It's just a game." Games have results, and results matter. The lesson is this: For almost everyone, losing is inevitable.

You're going to lose at some point, it's part of competing. Your commitment to Winning isn't to eliminate Losing. Your job is to minimize the downside when you lose, and then do everything possible to recover as quickly as possible after a loss.

On your road to Winning, every loss is like a dirty rest stop along the way. You don't always know when it's coming, but you know it will be part of the journey. It won't be pleasant, but you deal with it and wash your hands and get back on the road as quickly as you can.

That's why I have a huge issue with "participation trophies" for kids. I get it, kids like trophies. For a few bucks extra, you get a trophy *and* a hat. You don't have to show up for the practices or games, you'll be playing without a score, without accountability, without some recognition of actual achievement, but you're still getting that trophy. You finished in eleventh place. Everyone's a winner.

Seriously?

For very young kids, I understand and support the value of emphasizing the experience instead of the results. It's inclusive and supportive and gives children their first experience in sports. But by the time they're in first grade, it's acceptable—no, it's essential—to teach kids that sometimes they will lose, and then teach them *how* to lose. Teach them the value of working hard and achieving something. Teach them how it feels to put in effort and earn results. Teach them that a loss is the best way to learn to win.

Teach them that Winning matters. Results matter.

No one wants to see kids be disappointed. It's hard for the kid, and sometimes even harder for the parent. But those who can learn to handle it, and use it to grow instead of giving up, will be so much better prepared for life's challenges.

Because as they get older, they won't be receiving any participation trophies for just showing up. And the sooner they can learn to handle tough losses and disappointment, the less they'll fear adversity and failure.

The same is true for adults, isn't it? The more we

experience—and survive—big losses and disappointments, the more we realize how much we can handle—how strong and resilient we really are. Life requires you to show up, participate, play, keep score, recognize achievement... and even when you do all those things, you still don't always get the trophy.

But just because you lost doesn't mean you have *to be* lost. How close are you to reconnecting with Winning? A few inches? A mile? The length of a marathon? You must focus on the end of the race, not on the loss that just put a huge pothole in your path. The farther you wander from your course, the longer it will take to get back on track. That's how one loss becomes two, two becomes five, and now you're wandering deeper and deeper into hell with no way to find your way back.

MJ used to go ballistic on teammates who'd chatter about how the team was going to have a great game or a great season, because he knew they'd fall apart if the season got off to a bad start—and then he'd be carrying them. "How do you *know*?" he'd ask. "How you know we're gonna be great? We haven't done anything yet. What are you celebrating?"

I think about that every New Year's Eve, when people go crazy promising what a great year they're going to have. *I'm gonna kill it this year, I'm crushing it!* They start the year drunk, hungover, too tired to get up... but it's "their year." They haven't done one thing, have no real plans suggesting the new year will be any more productive and successful than the last, but they're already celebrating.

And by February, they feel that familiar fear of failure, and they give up. Again.

When you're truly resilient, giving up is never an option.

I've been blessed to know many champions, and I'm not talking about superstar athletes. These are ordinary people who are anything but ordinary, whose resilience has allowed them to accomplish amazing things, and face challenges and obstacles that seem insurmountable. They come from all walks of life, and totally diverse backgrounds, but they have one thing in common: They never give up.

I'm thinking about my friend Laval St. Germain, a Canadian commercial airline pilot and tremendous speaker, who climbed Mount Everest without the use of supplemental oxygen, and crossed the Atlantic Ocean in a solo rowboat in record-setting time. I'm thinking of the relentless Holly Hollis Stars, a brilliant and beautiful young attorney from Baton Rouge with the rarest and most aggressive form of breast cancer, who fights her battle and her fears every day with courage, grace, and unwavering faith in herself. I'm thinking about so many people I've met along the way—those who are fighting to take care of aging parents or sick children, fighting to make better lives for themselves and those they love, fighting their fears and limitations and everything that stands between them and Winning.

And I'm thinking about my father, Surjit Singh Grover, whose courage and resilience made me what I am today. I lost my dad in 2017, two days after Christmas and two days before his seventy-seventh birthday. I've known and been close to many great men, but none impacted my life more indelibly than he did. He wasn't famous, wasn't even a sports fan, and he didn't care about being social, but every day of his life was about Winning, for himself and those around him. From his decision to come to the US to raise his family, to watching his two sons and his many grandchildren grow up to make him proud, he lived every day with a vision of how to do things better, not just for himself but for the love of his life, my mother, Rattan, and for the whole family. He was a man of great faith, a proud Sikh who wore a turban and endured the prejudice that goes along with being "different." He loved a good dirty joke, saved forty years of newspaper clippings that mentioned my name, and never wavered in his belief that hard work and dedication were the answer to everything. I know he had fears about how he'd take care of everyone counting on him. But he had no doubts about his ability to do it.

His resilience became mine. And it's because of him I can share with you what I've learned. Rest in peace, Baba.

#1.
WINNING KNOWS
ALL YOUR SECRETS

Every night, somewhere between 2:00 and 4:00 a.m., I wake up and realize I am not alone.

No matter how dark the room, regardless of whether I'm at home or on the road, I wake up to hear someone talking to me. Sometimes several voices at once.

I don't even have to open my eyes to know who they are. I can feel them surrounding the bed, waiting to have a word with me.

And they never fucking go away.

Winning takes long walks in your head, usually in the middle of the night, and brings everyone you don't want to see. The skeletons in the closet. The monsters under the bed. Your secrets. Your fears. Your insecurities. Your doubts. You wake up in the darkness to thoughts and ideas and worries that you didn't have when you went to sleep, but suddenly there they are, blowing up your world.

You thought you were the only one, right?

You aren't alone. I know that many people have the

same experience, and won't talk about it. They think it makes them sound crazy, or weak, or scared. So I'm talking about it, because this nightly event shapes my thoughts and actions every day, and it has everything to do with how I approach Winning.

Your anxiety about the unknown future, the lies, the guilt, the feelings of inadequacy and failure, the fear of letting others down . . . most people are terrified by those late-night visits; they don't want to deal with that kind of mental isolation. So they wait miserably for the terror to pass, pretending nothing is wrong. They stuff those skeletons back in the closet, and hope no one ever finds out about the demons and secrets they keep hidden.

It doesn't work. You can get out of bed, turn on the lights, start your day, blast the TV, sing in the shower . . . but everywhere you go, there they are. There you are.

Winning is your nightmare even during the day.

And the more you try to keep those things hidden, the louder and wilder they get, until you can't see or hear anything else.

The chaos in your head may lessen during daylight, when you have other things to distract you; all those voices might finally shut up for a while. But the last thing you'll hear as they fade away at dawn is their hysterical laughter and daily warning: *We'll see you tonight.*

Winners crave that time alone in the dark. That's their time to think, to plan, to hear themselves, to talk with those ghosts in the room, and listen to the answers. They don't fear reality, they don't hide from the truth, and they're not afraid to confront their own flaws and weaknesses.

They open the closet, and give all those skeletons and demons their freedom.

I've been known to shake their hands, give them a hug, offer them a snack or stiff drink in the evening, while we break down our day and laugh about which of us fucked up the worst.

There is no greater superpower than the ability to say "This is who I am." Most people push that away, because they don't want to be judged. Winners don't care. They judge themselves, and live with the verdict.

Think about how much energy and time go into trying to be someone or something you're not. How much further along would you be if you put that same effort into being yourself? When you're confident in who you are, when you can stop worrying about what others think and finally decide what *you* think, you'll understand the relief and satisfaction of feeling those ghosts become a part of you. Possibly the best part of you.

Most people look outside themselves for help. They change jobs, teams, relationships, coaches, addresses, diets, routines, friends, hairstyles . . . anything that might help them reinvent who they are, as if new scenery will fix everything. As if their secrets will just disappear if no one else ever knows about them. They tell you they've changed, they're not that person anymore. False. You're *always* that person. You can change your habits, your surroundings, your looks, your attitude . . . but it's still you in there. And the longer you fight with that, the longer you're at war with yourself, the longer you'll struggle to find some peace.

Stop looking for others to save you. Your greatest partners and allies are already inside you, and they're talking to you all the time. Listen to those ghosts and skeletons. Join the conversation. Stop telling them they're wrong, and open your mind to the possibility—the truth—that they are 100 percent correct. Let them into your life, and tell them, *Let's do this together, I can't do this without you.* You need them. They need you. They *are* you, and they know you better than you know yourself.

They're your dark side, and they're your greatest power.

Of all the things I talked about in *Relentless*, none made people more agitated than my discussion of the dark side.

"Deep inside you," I wrote, "there's an undeniable force driving your actions, the part of you that refuses to be ordinary, the piece that stays raw and untamed. Not just instinct, but killer instinct. The kind you keep in the dark, where you crave things you don't talk about. And you don't care how it comes across to others, because you know this is who you are, and you wouldn't change if you could. . . .

"Your dark side is your fuel, your energy. It excites you, keeps you on the edge, recharges you, fills your tank. . . . It's an addiction as powerful as your addiction to success."

I got emails. Letters. Messages on social media. Interview requests. I had people come up to me at events just to pull me aside and whisper, "I need to talk to you about this dark side thing."

Note: The dark side isn't "a" thing. It's *the* thing.

They wanted to talk to me (privately, because no one wants to talk about this publicly) for one of two reasons: either they were worried, because they thought they didn't have a dark side, or they were relieved, because they'd known they had a dark side all along, and thought they were the only ones.

Neither of those things is true.

To be clear: When we talk about the dark side, we're not talking about evil, or *Star Wars*, or bad behavior, or Harry Potter (a personal favorite of Kobe's).

This is about what drives you. It's the place you go in your mind that allows you to leave everything else behind, and focus on one thing: Winning.

Everyone has a dark side. But not everyone can admit it. The CEO of a multibillion-dollar corporation asked me to speak to his entire company, and then got on stage to say he really didn't understand the whole dark side thing (lie) because he didn't have one (lie) and he had no secrets (lie lie lie). Afterward, at least a dozen of his employees came up to me to say the guy had the biggest dark side they'd ever seen. That was completely validated a few months later when he was kicked out of his own company for basically letting his dark side run the business into the ground.

The dark side has to be controlled, or it will control you.

I had the opportunity to work with the founder of a major restaurant chain, who hosted a dinner for me and fifty of his top people. Someone asked me to talk about the dark side, and its relevance to business success. I asked the group, "Who has the biggest dark side in this room?" And fifty people immediately looked at their founder.

To his credit, he laughed and accepted the compliment.

Kobe had a dark side that was so big it required its own personality: the Black Mamba. He created it when he was going through a difficult time personally and wanted a place he could go mentally, where he could continue to perform at the highest level professionally.

So he chose one of the most dangerous venomous snakes in the world to be his alter ego, after seeing the movie *Kill Bill*, which involved an assassin code-named Black Mamba, as well as an actual black mamba snake that was used to kill someone. Kobe saw that and thought, *That's me.* I don't know if he meant the assassin or the snake, probably both. And that's how the Black Mamba was born.

When he stepped across those lines onto the court, he became that deadly assassin, ready to strike at any moment without hesitation or fear. Until he left the arena after a game, he wasn't Kobe, with legal issues and family problems; he was the Mamba, and nothing could touch him. He could break from it when he was with his family, or occasionally when he needed to relax, but as soon as it was time to work, he was all Mamba again.

After he talked about it publicly, it was no surprise that everyone wanted to understand the Mamba Mentality so they could be just like Kobe.

Not possible.

Mamba Mentality is extreme beyond description. You can learn about it, you can study it, but it's almost impossible to imitate it. You have to *live it*, feel it, experience it—not just for a day or a week, but for years. It's a lifestyle, not an experiment. I've seen a lot of players try to reach that level of intensity and hyper focus. It has destroyed more careers than it's helped, because it's too intense to handle and too deadly to maintain. I don't know too many who achieved it, other than Kobe himself.

That's the transformative power of the dark side. It will take you where you want to go, if you allow it.

But it has to come from within you, because the dark side is personal to each individual. It's the result of everything you've won and lost, your disappointments, your fears, your achievements.

Your dark side is a song that only you can hear, if you have the courage to listen for it.

For some, its origin is easy to identify: Getting cut from the team, and committing your life to becoming the best player in history. Losing your job, and starting a rival company that puts your competition out of business. Growing up poor, and vowing you'll never live that way again.

For others, the dark side is very deep and private. Living with health issues. Losing a loved one. Suffering abuse. Growing up without one of your parents. Being told you'll never succeed at anything.

Everyone has that secret wound that never heals, that skeleton they can't get rid of. Maybe you were the fat kid who was teased, the poor student who barely finished school, the child with a speech impediment who was ashamed to speak in front of the class.

I can tell you right here, I was the fat kid. My mother, Rattan, loved to feed us, because when you come from India, food isn't always plentiful. She and my dad took great pleasure in providing for us because it was something they didn't have when they were kids. I took full advantage of that.

And I wasn't just fat, I also wasn't athletic. When we had to take the physical fitness tests in elementary school, I couldn't do the pull-ups or push-ups. But there was one thing I could do: sit-ups. I could go all day if they let me, just to show that I could. My whole body would be on fire, but I was going to own those sit-ups. I couldn't hop over the pommel horse or climb the rings, but this thing with the sit-ups, that worked for me.

I still remember how it felt to be that kid. And if you're wondering: Everything changed my freshman year of high school. I was already sick of being out of shape and overweight, and I was feeling the rumblings of a dark side that wanted me to do something about it. I decided to play basketball, for a coach who ran our asses into the ground. That, combined with the two hours it took to get back and forth to school every day, left me with no time to sit around eating and watching TV; my new world was all about school and basketball. The weight came off fast and I was suddenly an athlete.

I got even closer to my dark side a few years later, when I tore up my ACL playing college basketball at the University of Illinois-Chicago. Instead of having the proper surgery to repair it—which would have meant missing a season and losing my scholarship—I settled for a procedure to just clean it up so I could rush back, wearing a huge metal brace. It worked in the short term, but left me with a lifetime of orthopedic issues, and ensured that my basketball career wouldn't last long.

And because of that, I decided to devote my life to helping other athletes, which worked out pretty well.

But those things stay with you. And they can be your greatest fuel, if you choose to use them that way.

If you really want to identify the source of your dark side, try this:

Take all the disappointments in your life—everyone who said no, everyone who teased you, every job you lost, every game you lost, every time someone said you weren't good enough, every relationship that ended badly—and imagine laying them all in front of you. Just spread them out all over an imaginary table.

Now: Hold your hand over each one, mentally reconnecting with how each made you feel. Warm… nauseous… cold … nothing … *radioactive hot*. That's the one. That's your fuel. The one that burns you without even having to touch it . . . that's your dark side fuel. That's Iron Man's armor, Wonder Woman's bracelets, Captain America's shield, Spider-Man's web, Superman's cape, Thor's hammer, Batman's mask. That's what's driving you, and that's your superpower.

People are afraid to get close to all that hurt and disappointment, because they open themselves up to reliving it, and that's rarely pleasant. But you must be willing to look at it, relive it, and embrace it, before you can draw power from it. If you can't face your own truth, if you can't deal with the darkest part of your past, you'll never be able to change your story.

Tapping into the dark side isn't about revenge or anger, it's not an FU to everyone who ever hurt you; that's an emotional distraction, not fuel. The dark side is about total focus and tunnel vision on what's in front of you, not a million untamed emotions about things that happened in your lifetime. Those things are there, they're always with you, but when you're chasing a win, all your focus needs to be on that win.

Tom Brady didn't start on his high school JV team, he had to battle to start at Michigan, and he was the 199th pick in the sixth round of his NFL draft. He has said many times how he never forgets that he was drafted after six other quarterbacks. He has a production company called "199 Productions," just to make sure you know he never forgets. But you can be sure that when he's on the field competing, he's not thinking about it, and he's not talking about it. He just has to win, and the revenge takes care of itself.

You're not trying to prove others wrong, you're proving yourself right.

In *Relentless*, I talked in depth about how to identify your dark side, your alter ego. I explained how to control it, and not be afraid of it, how to harness its power to create unlimited fuel and energy.

In this book, we're taking it to the next level. We have no choice. Because Winning makes your dark side even darker.

Why? Because to *keep on* winning, the darkness has to be ever stronger, until there is virtually no light, there are no shadows, and you have to trust yourself enough to feel your way in the darkness. You'll need everything within you to survive the repeat journey to Winning, and that means no holding back. You're leaving behind all the inhibitions, the suppressed feelings, the self-consciousness, the images of everyone who said you won't make it. Your new traveling companions—the skeletons, the ghosts, the demons—are no longer your enemies, they're your dark side partners. They fly only first class, stay in the finest hotels, drink only top-shelf booze, and make you pay for it all, which you gladly do, because Winning is worth it. They're going to be there anyway, so you may as well laugh with them, cry with them, get pissed off with them, have those talks with them in the middle of the night.

Kobe loved anything to do with the dark side. We had that in common, and he loved knowing he could talk with me about it. One night after a road game we went out for a drink in the hotel bar, and somehow we started talking about what it would be like to hang out with our dark sides. Across the bar, there were two guys who obviously recognized Kobe, saw two empty chairs at our table, and came over to ask if they could join us. Kobe looked at me, looked at them, and said, "These seats are taken."

The guys looked around, a little offended, and said, "There's no one else in here."

"There's someone sitting there," I responded. "Right now."

I'm sure they figured we were drunk and walked away.

Spend some time with you dark side partners, your demons, skeletons, and ghosts. They make the best drinking buddies.

Trust them to bring you to Winning's doorstep; they know exactly how to get there, and they'll take you there, if you let them.

Because Winning sure as hell isn't coming to you.

Winning doesn't meet you at the start of your race; it hates crowds. It meets you near the finish, when the others have quit or failed. Until that point, Winning has no interest. *Let me know when you're serious*, it says, and *then we'll talk*.

Winning introduces you to yourself for the first time. It forces you to be honest about who you really are, what you really want, and what you're willing to do to get it. It makes you challenge your own values, and compromise your relationships and promises and commitments when you realize they're standing in your way.

It waits for your dark side to become darker.

The dark side is about taking care of yourself; it protects you and satisfies you, and *only* you. The *darker* side allows you to impact and influence others to create action, elevate and believe in themselves. This is the trademark of a winner: someone with power who empowers others as well, the way MJ helped Kobe throughout his career, Kobe helped Wade, Wade helped LeBron, LeBron helps others. True power is shared.

The dark side puts you in the driver's seat. The *darker* side allows you to drive from wherever you want to sit.

The dark side is somewhere you visit alone, in secret,

when you need that extra level of power and strength and release. Sorry, no other visitors allowed. The *darker* side is with you all the time, and you're not afraid to show it.

The dark side allows you to use your abilities to their fullest. The *darker* side—and this is key—compensates for the abilities you don't have.

The dark side tells you it's okay to have three drinks, because you've earned it. Your *darker* side tells you to stop at one. Not because you can't handle more, but because you don't need it.

The dark side wins battles. Your *darker* side wins the war.

The dark side makes you angry, angry at yourself, because you hesitated in life. The *darker* side realizes anger is a waste of energy.

The dark side makes you a hero. The *darker* side makes you a villain. And everyone loves a true villain.

Your dark side gives you the power and courage to give Winning what it wants. Your *darker* side allows you to use it.

When you get knocked down, your dark side tells you to get up and fight. But it's your *darker* side that tells you to stay down for a while, until you really understand what went wrong so you can get back up stronger. *Remember this feeling*, it tells you, *remember this cold frozen bloody battleground, because we're never going to be here again.*

The *darker* side is your standing eight count in life, and it can last as long as you need it to . . . minutes, weeks, maybe years. But when you get back up, you'll be at full power and ready to fight.

Your dark side is about what you want to do, what you want for yourself. Your *darker* side is about action. It doesn't want to hear what you're planning, it wants to see what you accomplish. You're going to have a great season. You're going to write a book. You're going to travel or paint or make a million dollars. Fine. Show me. Stop talking about it. The *darker* you get, the quieter you need to be, so your results can do the talking for you.

Your *darker* side takes you from the dream to the reality. Instead of imagining yourself singing on stage, you get your ass on the stage and actually sing. You might be terrible, you might get booed off the stage, you might get a standing ovation, but something is going to happen. You've released something inside you that says, *Hey, I can do this!* And your *darker* side slaps you on the back of your head and says, *You dumb MF, I've been saying this your whole life!*

The *darker* side is an elite private club no one knows about. You can't apply for it, but everyone knows who the other members are. You see that other person coming, and you just know. Dark sees dark, like an invisible aura that clings to you. You can't fake it.

Greater darkness requires greater isolation. Winners make decisions alone, and they deal with the backlash alone. They worry alone. They work alone. And they feel alone, even when they're surrounded by millions.

If you have a problem being alone, we need to change that.

Like being "selfish," being "alone" is a powerful condition with a bad reputation.

All of the greats I've worked with—MJ, Kobe, Dwyane, Scottie, Charles, Hakeem, and so many others—understood the power of isolation. Not just as the inability to go out in public places for fear of causing a security issue, but as a mental state. No matter how many fans and cameras followed them around—regardless of how many were always watching their every move—they knew a huge part of their success was the ability to be mentally alone.

Same for the executives and entrepreneurs I work with; each has a method for creating space and silence around himself or herself. The insurance executive who starts her day before the family gets up, so she has a couple of hours to think and plan without interruption . . . the pharmaceutical CEO who built a private gym for himself so he can work out in total solitude . . . the music producer who learned to fly his own airplane so he can literally take off and get away . . . they all crave silence and solitude. That's their time to think, to plan, to escape the noise and chaos and demands of the outside world.

Winning teaches you isolation. Because no one can understand what you're going through.

As I said at the beginning of this discussion: Winners crave time alone in the dark.

For Michael, solitude gave him a break from his own relentless pursuit of perfection and excellence in everything he did, as well as the countless people trying to get near him and talk to him and just look at him. Isolation made all of that go away, if only for a brief time.

If that sounds good to you, if you really want some time alone away from everything and everyone else, try it sometime, not just for a day or two, but for weeks and months.

Everyone thinks they can be alone until it's time to be alone.

Those who can do it have the strongest dark sides imaginable. Their secrets are their companions, their support system.

Because no matter how many people will contribute to your wins, in the end it's all about you. Your preparation. Your confidence. Your commitment. Your grip on your emotions. Your partnership with the voices in your head.

If any of those things falters, most likely so will you.

Stop lying to yourself about who you are, and why you're that way. That's your fuel, not something to hide. You can't win until you embrace this.

#1.
WINNING NEVER LIES

A few years ago, I was approached by the parents of a rookie superstar, who wanted me to work with their son. He had everything going for him: high draft pick, big contract, great shoe deal, lots of endorsements.

One problem: His performance was mediocre at best, his team was losing, and people were starting to use the B word about him. Bust.

I guess that's three problems, with more to come. When you're not winning, those problems start to pile up quickly.

The kid had talent, but it wasn't materializing into results. He was the first one in the team's facility every day, working out at dawn and posting about it on his social media. He had a cute girlfriend. He had two cute dogs. He carried a Bible. He did more community events and charity functions than anyone on the team, and he posted about those too. His family told me he was going to be the next Muhammad Ali, changing the world and becoming the greatest to ever play his sport.

If he could just win.

So I sat down with him and we just started talking. He

had all the right things to say: *I just want to win. I'm going to have my best season ever. This team can do great things. I'll do whatever you tell me.* All the standard bull that sounds right but means nothing unless you can back it up.

I wanted so badly to hear him say: *I'm messed up. I'm confused. And I don't know what to do about it.*

I can't fix perfect. But I can fix messed up.

After a half hour of asking direct questions, and getting weak answers, I changed course.

"Go home," I told him. "We're going to meet again tomorrow, and here's what I need you to do before then."

His assignment: Go sit somewhere alone—no family or agents or teammates or friends—and ask yourself: What's real, and what's fake? Are you healthy? Are you scared? Are you mad at someone? Write it down. Write a whole list if you get going. But you need to find out what's true and what's an act, because something is getting in your way.

I figured there was a fifty-fifty chance he'd come back, and a 10 percent chance he'd come back with a list. But there he was the next day, with notes he'd typed in his phone, and he was rocked.

Everything was fake. He didn't trust the people around him. He didn't trust the team. He didn't trust himself. He doubted his ability. He smoked weed and was afraid to get caught. He had multiple relationships and was afraid all these women in his life would find out about each other. He was worried about letting down his family and ruining his image. He had so many things in his head and in his life I don't know how he remembered to tie his shoes.

I told him the truest thing I know, and maybe you've

heard me say it: To have what you really want, you first must be who you really are.

How can you have any degree of mental clarity with all that chaos in your head?

And we went to work. As much as we worked on his body and his game, we worked on taking out some of the mental trash he'd piled up, flexing his IDGAF muscle so he could stop feeling guilty and "bad" about everything, and clear his mind of the lies he was telling himself and others.

At first, his performance actually got worse; he was trying so hard not to think about all the things he was getting rid of that for a while he couldn't think about anything else. But he was determined to work through it, and when I heard him tell his parents he didn't want to be Muhammad Ali, he just wanted to be himself, I knew we'd turned the corner. And his performance reflected that as well.

Winning knows the truth. And it needs you to admit it.

You can fake a lot of things. You can fake being happy, you can fake being successful, you can fake having a great relationship, you can fake confidence and knowledge and just about everything else. But you can't fake Winning.

Because even if you can fool absolutely everyone else . . . *you* still know the truth.

Winning is an absolute. There's a score, a dollar sign, a grade, a number on the scale. Even when your win isn't measured by the numbers—coming back from an injury, starting a new business, having a difficult conversation, getting a promotion, taking a vacation for the first time in years, going down a size in your clothes—there's something tangible that measures your result. It doesn't matter how hard you worked, how many hours you spent at the gym or office, how talented you are, how you sacrificed. Did you win?

We have so many ways of lying to ourselves. *The score was closer than it looked. The game was closer than the score. The team isn't as bad as its record. We saw some good things. We're headed in the right direction. This is our year.*

No. The score is the score. The number on the balance sheet is the number. Your grade is your grade. The scale is accurate. You took that vacation or you stayed home talking about it.

For too many people, it's easier to fake success than achieve it. All their energy goes into looking like a winner, instead of doing the work to actually *be* a winner.

I see athletes who start every season talking about how they've never been healthier, they've been in the gym every day at 4:00 a.m., this was the best off-season ever, these are the greatest teammates ever, they're going to win it all. And when they don't win it all, they're the first guys talking about how they're going to win it all the next season.

Stop talking. When you accomplish something, Winning will do all your talking for you.

I'm sure you know people who brag about getting up at 4:00 a.m., as if that's the trademark of success. For some, it can be; they consistently use that time to be productive and focused and it's an established part of their Winning routine.

But for many, it's just another photo op for social media. "Let's get it!" "Gotta beat the sun!" "This is how you crush the competition!" Honestly, every time I hear that, I think two things: Either those people need to find some- one who makes them want to stay in bed a little longer, or they're running from something—likely, themselves—and they have to get out of bed as early as possible so they can stop staring at the ceiling thinking about all their worries and fears and everything they're faking. Either way, when you're up before dawn and the first thing you do is post a video of your alarm going off at 4:23 a.m., that's not about you focusing on the day, it's about you focusing on every- one else and how you can impress them.

Every single day, I get messages and emails from people—not clients, these are regular people I generally don't know—sending me videos and pictures of them- selves working out at 4:00 a.m. I have no idea why. I assume they're looking for congratulations and "You got this!" But honestly, who cares if you're in the gym at 4:00 a.m. or 4:00 p.m. or any other time? Did you get results? Are you achieving something? Tell me what you accomplished, and how it's helping you win. Until then, I just want to tell them to get more sleep.

How did sleep deprivation become a symbol of ambi- tion? When did "rest" become the equivalent of "lazy"? How did "so busy" become a symbol of importance? If you can't get enough sleep, it's not a badge of honor; it's a weakness that shows you're not getting enough done dur- ing the day. Occasionally, yes, you're going to lose sleep in exchange for a win. But as a lifestyle, as a way to show how important and busy you are, you end up looking like a scatterbrain who can't get your life together.

Winning exposes you in every way. Every lie you told yourself and others, everything you faked and flaunted — Winning holds it up to the brightest light for everyone to see. It rips your mask off, and shows everyone what you knew all along: This ain't that. You haven't won anything yet.

If "fake it till you make it" is your strategy for success, you have very little chance of making it. Does it make you feel good to show off a huge house or car you don't really own or can't afford? If you're really helping others and doing good things in the world, are others talking about the results, or are you the only one talking? Are you proud of the million fake followers you bought? It might get you started, but if you can't back it up soon, you're just a fake who didn't make it.

Especially if you're starting to believe what you're selling to everyone else.

You already know what you're faking to others. Do you know what you're faking to yourself? Are you honest about your effort and commitment? Are you showing up, not just physically but 100 percent mentally?

One of the worst "motivational" expressions ever: "Showing up is half the battle."

No. Showing up is *none* of the battle. If it's a battle for you to just show up, you're so far from Winning you won't find it with GPS and a team of hunting dogs.

Winning demands you show up with purpose and intention and discipline. When someone says, "Showing up is half the battle," you're looking at an individual who is already losing that battle.

I'm not even talking about physically dragging your-self into your workout or your classes or your career; if that's consistently a struggle for you, you're dealing with entry-level issues that have nothing to do with Winning.

I'm talking about being mentally engaged and focused on what you're doing—not half the time but *all* the time.

Why? Because Winning is going to show up. It's show-ing up today, and tomorrow, and every day after that. It shows up regardless of bad moods and bad news and bad weather, it doesn't care what else is going on. It doesn't have to decide whether to show up at 40 percent or 90 per-cent. It doesn't care if you show up at all, because you're expendable; if you can't summon the desire and energy to make it, someone else will.

Winning shows up ready to play. Your obligation is to meet it there, and leave your bullshit excuses behind: *It's not the right time. I need to think about it. I'm not ready. It might rain. It's too expensive. Things are too tense at home.*

Winning doesn't care what you're dealing with; it doesn't care what excuses you can invent. It doesn't want to hear what stopped you and why, whether you had a bad day, whether things are rough at home. Winning isn't interested. It expects you to show up and deal with your problems on your own time.

Winning loves a good storm just to see how you'll deal with the high winds and freezing rain and blistering heat, all at once, because this storm isn't outside in the street, it's in your head. The sun can be shining and you're lost in a mental blizzard.

But you still have to show up.

How many times have you not shown up because no one agreed with what you were doing? What haven't you done because you couldn't find a partner and didn't want to ride alone? Every excuse you've come up with, every time you've shown up halfway or not at all, you've slid further and further from what you're chasing.

Showing up is in your control, in every way. It means being present—physically and mentally—when you'd rather be doing something else. Putting your long-term goals ahead of short-term pleasures, and controlling those pleasures for the long run. Staying in the race when you're hurting and struggling. Because one day you won't be able to show up, and it won't be your choice.

Showing up is knowing that the life we've been given is temporary. Tomorrow is here permanently. So is Winning. We are not.

Showing up means knowing you have *this* moment, not worrying about yesterday, because yesterday isn't worrying about you, and it's not coming to look for you today.

Showing up is accepting that everyone struggles, and realizing that "everyone" means you, because if no one else shows up, it's still your responsibility.

Showing up is knowing the day you're about to have isn't the day you planned. Few are.

Showing up means you're probably showing up alone, and preferring it that way.

And above all, it means facing reality and embracing the truth about where you are in your life—because Winning never lies.

But most people do.

You may not lie about your age or weight or where you went last night or how many cookies you ate, but to some degree, we all lie to ourselves about something.

It's not my place to tell you what you're lying about to yourself, but you probably already know. And until you can stop the bullshit and start dealing with your own reality, you're going to be stuck exactly where you are, pretending you're a fine wine when everyone thinks you're a cork.

I'm talking to people who think of themselves as Ferraris, when everyone else sees them as scooters. They wear Gucci shoes, but have $12 in their pocket until payday. They dress in Armani and tell story after story about the big deals they brokered, without mentioning that those particular deals closed ten years ago. They've been trying to drop the same eight pounds for a decade.

And the biggest lie of all: "I have plenty of time."

You don't. None of us do.

Winning doesn't buy your lies. It's not impressed. You can tell people and show people whatever you want. Winning knows. And it thinks you're ridiculous.

You might be struggling, clawing, and manipulating to stay aboveground. But being a fraud won't help you succeed. Your story will crack. Your inconsistencies will show through. And you'll realize—too late—that all the energy you've invested in your imaginary image was spent on the wrong thing.

I used to have a huge intern program (I don't run one now, so don't ask), and I'm proud to say that today, many of the individuals who worked for me are among the world's top trainers and coaches in the NBA, NFL, MLB, NHL, collegiate sports, and even in Hollywood. My best interns were the guys who'd come in early, stay late, pick up towels, and do things without being asked or told. They came to us without living arrangements, without other obligations, without any motives except a sincere desire to learn and contribute. On the other hand, we had guys who were just *impressed*. Impressed with themselves, impressed to be around the athletes, impressed by who they knew and how they could use it. They could only stay for a week because they had a vacation planned. They needed us to provide housing (we didn't). They wanted to negotiate their pay.

I'd ask them a question and they'd answer, "I guess." You guess? I don't need you to guess, I can guess on my own. I need you to care enough to find out. You're looking at that phone all day—can you use it to find the answers I need? I wanted to grab some of these kids and shake them, lean in, and say: "Are you here to contribute, or to see what you can take away? You're telling me what you need, but what are you willing to *give*? Don't tell me you want to 'pick my brain,' or that you can really learn from me. I *know* that. What can I learn from *you*? And how can my clients benefit from the fact that I let you in the door?"

Those who stayed with us knew exactly what they wanted. They weren't in it for the money or the thrill of being around the superstars. They weren't weighing their options or deciding if the hard work and long hours were "worth it." They weren't looking for a Plan B. They were already living their Plan A.

When you're serious about Winning, every plan has to

be Plan A. You don't have the luxury of lying to yourself about all your other options. They don't exist.

A few years ago, I spoke to a major college football program and asked the players to share what was going through their minds the night before a big game. Every kid talked about visualizing the plays, getting in the zone, preparing for battle alongside their brothers. Typical pre-game pep talk clichés.

Then one young man spoke, and I'll never forget what he told his teammates: "I pray that I don't mess up," he said, "because this is all I have. I have no other option, I need to go to the pros. People are counting on me. *I'm counting on me.*"

He wasn't thinking about a backup plan—he wasn't considering a Plan B. He lived and worked every day to be sure he wouldn't need a Plan B. He didn't. He was drafted in the first round and went on to his next Plan A—as a starter in the NFL.

That's how winners execute.

Too many options = too many excuses, too many ways to get stuck. *Should I do this? Or that? Maybe this is better? What do you think?* You're so busy fabricating options that you can't make a decision. It's a simple choice: You can fail or you can succeed. Pick one. Act on it.

I have a corporate client who owns multiple auto dealerships, enjoys good food and good wine, and also struggles to keep his weight under control. When he's out to dinner, he sends me screenshots of menus. "Can I have this?" he asks. He knows not to start with "Can I substitute this or change that?" He's asking, plain and simple, what can he eat? Prepared how? I give him one answer, and I don't negotiate. You want to lose weight, here's what you have to do. You don't need the almond-crusted fish with fancy sauce; you can have grilled fish plain. No cookies. No fruit for now. "Bananas?" he asks. Deep breath from me: "I just said 'No fruit.' Drop some weight and then we'll talk about bananas."

When we started together, he said, "I'd like to have more options."

"You want options?" I asked. "Okay. You have the option of losing weight or gaining weight. Let me know."

The more options you add, the less likely you are to get the desired result. You already know what to do, and then you decide to get creative and start "tweaking." I hate tweaking. Tweaking just means: *Let me see how I can cheat a little here or there, make it a little easier, give myself an out. I already had the right answer, but let me see how I can screw this up.*

The greats aren't asking for options. They already know the choice: Win or don't win.

I'm not inflexible. If there's room to adapt and a reason to make small changes, we'll do that. But being tired of grilled fish isn't going to be the reason.

For my athletes, sticking with Plan A can involve everything from how often they need to get in an ice bath to when and what they can drink. I live in the real world, I'm not telling adults they can't have a drink. But I do ask questions that require them to take a stand: Can you drink the clear tequila instead of the brown tequila? Can you leave out the mixers and syrups? Yes? Okay. The greater the player, the more latitude there is for variations, because their abilities will compensate for indulgences. Most players don't qualify.

It works the same in the business world with bosses who want to keep their employees happy. These days I speak to a lot of businesses that want their teams to develop a winning mentality. They want their people to be tough and focused and driven, yet they somehow feel obligated to load up the team with every possible perk and option so everyone is happy. I understand the benefit of creating a certain kind of culture, but let it be a culture that rewards success, not the need for perks. If your people are showing up principally because you have a basketball court and free cookies on Fridays, you have the wrong people around you.

Here's my suggestion for every team, organization, and business that wants to keep people honest and accountable: create a WTF—"What the Fuck"—Department. The WTF Department functions as the in-house BS detector, with total authority to override management and HR, and put people in check for whatever they're faking. An employee is complaining to everyone that he deserves a raise and promotion, but his sales are the lowest on the team? WTF will point that out. Someone is upset because she didn't get a pat on the back for doing something she was supposed to do? WTF is there to remind her: *You're supposed to do that, it's your job.* The boss spends most of his workday making TikTok videos? WTF will be stopping by.

Be your own WTF Department. Hold yourself accountable. If you're not winning, if you're going to bed every night and waking up the next day hoping things will be better, if you're spending more time creating a false image of yourself as a winner than investing in ways to stop being a loser, it's time to drink up the truth. It will have a very bitter taste, but it will be worth it.

Because there's a long race ahead of you with no end in sight.

#1.

WINNING IS NOT A MARATHON, IT'S A SPRINT WITH NO FINISH LINE

At the beginning of this book, we talked about the "language of winning" and some of the idiotic expressions that mean nothing, slow you down, and end up knocking you right out of the race. I intentionally saved one of these clichés until now, because it's so wrong and misguided that it's getting its own chapter.

"It's a marathon, not a sprint!"

Stop it.

I'm sure this means something to someone, because people use it all the time to identify a dramatically challenging long-term journey, a prolonged mission that requires tremendous patience.

To me, it's about procrastination, uncertainty, and a total lack of focus.

Folks: You don't have that much time.

If you want to win, a marathon *is* a sprint.

You want to debate this with me? First do this: Get on a treadmill and try to run a mile in under five minutes.

That's a slower pace than the top marathoners would run, but close enough to make a point. They do it for 26.2 miles. I'm asking you for one.

Then come back and tell me whether it felt like a marathon or a sprint, if you can still stand up and breathe.

You get my point? Competitive marathoners push the entire distance. At no point do they say, "Eh, it's a marathon, I can take my time here." They may change speeds along the way, but to win a marathon, to even finish near the top, they're going hard for 26.2 miles.

And yes, you can finish a marathon without ever sprinting, you can go at your own pace, and it's still a great accomplishment. But we're talking about Winning here, not just finishing.

Every team finishes the season. Only one will win the title.

When people use the marathon/sprint line, they're usually trying to say, *Pace yourself, you have a long way to go.* That may be true, but more likely, it just rationalizes an excuse. *Slow down. What's the rush? Take your time. Don't overdo it.*

Usually, the people who use that line have never run a race of any kind, and certainly not a marathon. They want you to go as slow as they do, so they can feel better about their own lack of progress.

And while they're taking their time, going slow, pacing out that long marathon, someone else just sprinted past them and grabbed their dream.

No matter how long the distance, you have to treat every step as if it's the most important, because it is. In a real race, you don't have the luxury of stopping at the water station for five minutes. You run right through it, grab a cup as you go, and keep moving.

What the hell does it mean when people say, "It's about the journey, not the destination"? If you don't care about the destination, why take the journey? Just so you can wander around, dreaming about what might happen if you ever get somewhere? You don't run a race for the journey, you run it to arrive.

Whatever you're chasing in life, it's not an option to sit back, skip a few days, think about it for a month, and see how you feel in a year. It means doing it consistently, with purpose and focus, from start to finish. And when you get to the finish, you should already see the next starting gate in front of you. That's how a marathon becomes a series of sprints.

Winning has all the time in the world. You don't.

Technology, science, communication, transportation . . . everything in our world is moving faster, and it's not enough to just keep up; you have to move ahead.

Maybe you've heard the other dumb expressions along these lines: "Rome wasn't built in a day!"

No, it wasn't. It was built every day, for thousands and thousands of days.

That's how champions and competitors win. They deliver every day for thousands and thousands of days.

How about this one: "It's just one game." If that somehow makes you feel better after a loss, you don't deserve to win. It's "just one game" . . . until you miss the playoffs or lose the season by just one game.

Just one game . . . just one meeting . . . just an idea . . . just a mistake.

Translation: *It's not that important. I have plenty of time.*

No, you don't.

Take out that one little word "just" and the whole meaning changes.

It's one game. *You're not getting it back. It mattered.*

It's a meeting. *If others are taking the time to participate, contribute something of value.*

It's an idea. *Work with it, don't overthink it or dismiss it.*

It's a mistake. *Admit it. Own it. Don't repeat it.*

Winning's unforgiving race doesn't allow you the luxury of shortcuts and procrastination. It wants to see you sprinting.

Kobe sprinted through life like no one I've ever known.

He had no hobbies or distractions. Didn't play golf, didn't hang out with buddies, didn't go to parties. Occasionally, he'd decide to see a movie and would rent out the whole theater so he could take a small group of friends or family to see it privately, usually twice in a row. Otherwise, he trained. He practiced. He studied film. Besides his beautiful family, which was his top non-basketball priority, his entire focus centered on one obsession: Winning.

For twenty years in the NBA, Kobe sprinted from season to season, game to game, quarter to quarter. He never slowed down, and he couldn't comprehend those who did. He'd hear about a group of players heading to a concert or a party or another sporting event, and he'd rarely join them. *You go ahead and do that*, he thought. *I'll be right here doing this.* That was his time to elevate himself, to do the work others weren't doing. He believed the extra work added years of advantage and experience to his skill set.

He had no patience for waiting or rebuilding. He began and ended every season the same way: racing toward a championship.

Even when he retired in 2016, he kept up the same pace—with new obsessions—and had more wins in his forty-one years than most people could accomplish in several lifetimes. A remarkable life, with remarkable achievements. Which led many to ask: How was he able to achieve so much in the time he was given?

Kobe's secret weapon: He had the unfaltering ability to focus on what he was doing, for as long as he needed to, until he got the results he wanted.

Most people worry about how long something will take. Winners just keep going until it gets done.

Kobe didn't measure time; he didn't care how long it would take or what else he had to do. He only cared about whether it would contribute to his results. It didn't matter to him if we were in the gym at 3:00 a.m. or 3:00 p.m. He didn't know how many years he'd play, he just knew how many rings he wanted. He didn't have a timetable for writing a bestselling book or producing an Oscar-winning film, he just wanted it done. *Now.*

You can't achieve that level of success by wondering how much time you have. You can only focus on the results, and keep sprinting toward greatness until you're forced to stop.

It took death to make Kobe stop.

In the words of Kobe's great friend and mentor Michael Jordan: "I've never lost a game. I just ran out of time."

Most people never think about running out of time. They look ahead and see days and months and years of empty dates on the calendar, and assume they have plenty of time to fill them.

Kobe's success wasn't the result of managing his time. It was the result of his relentless focus on results.

We allow time to dictate so many of our decisions. *How long will it take? When is it due? How much time should I put in? It's late, I need to stop. What time does this end?*

Stop managing time, and start managing your focus.

Winning doesn't care if you have time. It expects you to *make* time, because nothing is more important.

Attaining your dream is about managing results, not managing the clock.

I know there are countless books and experts and theories on time management. I understand the value of scheduling and organizing and fighting procrastination. It's a great form of discipline.

Of course, if you were more focused, you wouldn't be procrastinating, and you'd already be disciplined.

Time is undefeated. No matter what you do, it will outlast you, outsmart you, and paralyze you—if you allow it to.

You can't control it. But you can control its hold on you . . . by controlling your focus on the end result.

Think about it: You're working on something that has to be completed by the end of the day. You feel pressure. You're watching the clock. A voice in your head keeps saying, *Come on, come on, what's taking so long?* You have four hours left. Next time you look, you have three hours left. You've received seven emails asking when you'll be done. Two hours left, and you're nowhere near finished. You get up, go to the bathroom, get a snack, check your phone, again. Tick tick tick . . . you're stressed and distracted. With an hour left, you're rushing, making mistakes, and taking shortcuts. You know it's not your best work. It might be your worst work ever.

But you got it done "on time." Congrats.

How would this have played out if you were focused on the work, instead of how long it was taking?

Winning requires results. And results require focus.

Turn off your phone. Turn off the TV. Close your door. You don't need to ask eight people what to do. It's just you and the work now. No distractions, no clock. Focus on what you're doing, not what you're missing. You control everything.

And when you're finished, you'll have achieved the results in half the time, and doubled the quality.

Is it easy? No. Winning never is. But those who can master this type of focus will separate themselves from everyone else in the race.

You can practice this, by the way. Start training yourself to experience what focus really feels like. Simple exercise: Do something with the opposite hand. Eat, write, throw a ball, swing a bat, brush your teeth. Something you do all the time that's completely automatic with your dominant hand. You don't think about the mechanics of brushing your teeth, it requires no focus. But try it with the opposite hand . . . it's awkward and uncomfortable and requires massive focus to execute. You're fighting your brain to stay locked in on this simple task. Can you do it for thirty seconds? A minute? Can you go longer? I'm not comparing wielding your toothbrush to sprinting a marathon, but if you can't control this, how are you going to manage that?

Here's another way to retrain your mind: Count up to a deadline, not down. Time forces you to count down to the finish: *5 . . . 4 . . . I have so much left to do . . . 3 . . . hurry up, I'm running out of time . . . 2 . . . I'm not going to make it . . . 1. Time's up. The clock ran out.*

Focus counts up. The numbers are infinite, and the clock never runs out. *1 . . . 2 . . . Here's what's ahead to reach the goal . . . 3 . . . Let's get started . . . 4 . . . Stop counting and just do the work.*

It's not about how much time you have left, it's about how much you can still do in the minutes, hours, weeks, and months that remain. Instead of counting down to the end of the calendar—and blowing off December because of holidays and parties and year-end fatigue—count each and every day that you can still accomplish something before the end of the year, as everyone else checks out. When you count up, you never get to zero, so you never lose momentum; you can start the new year at full strength, while everyone else tries to remember where they left off.

Time tells you what you didn't accomplish. Focus turns off the clock and directs all your energy to the result.

If you're focusing on a time limit, you can't focus on the moment. Time pressure kills performance—*if your* mind can't block it out. You see this all the time in sports — for example, a quarterback folding under pressure or a basketball player who can't take the last shot. They start counting down in their heads, instead of executing. Most players are painfully aware that the clock is running out, and they panic: *I've got three seconds, I gotta get this shot off.* They're so distracted that they overthink, make careless mistakes, and lose control of the moment.

The greats are always in the moment: If MJ or Kobe had three seconds on the clock, they weren't thinking, *Can I do this in three seconds? Do I have enough time?* They knew *exactly* what they could accomplish in three seconds; their focus was strictly on getting the job done. *Three seconds? Get me to that spot, I got this. One: I'm here. Two: I'm there. Three: basket.*

Even the score counts up.

Focus is the ultimate weapon in the war on time. While time is trying to get in your face, waving its arms and setting off alarms to remind you how late you are, focus takes you to that place where you have no idea how much time has passed, and you don't care.

Time reminds you how much you didn't get done. Focus locks you in, until you finish.

Time tells you to stop what you're doing and get some sleep. Focus tells you there's more to do. You can sleep when the job is done.

Time pressure is external. Focus comes from inside you, where no one else can control it.

Time creates distractions. Focus blocks them out.

Time tells you to hurry. Focus tells time to STFU.

When you're managing time, all you can see is how long it will take. When you're managing focus, you don't care.

Time is about others. Focus is all about you.

Ever been in total focus mode? You start something and realize hours later that you haven't moved, eaten, peed . . . you have no idea if the earth is still turning. You don't know if its noon or midnight. You're just locked in on what you're doing.

When I'm with an athlete, everything else falls away. I'm not thinking that I also need to go to Costco and walk my dog and answer my email. I'm concentrating on what we're doing and what we need to do next. I might be counting how many steps he's taking, whether he's landing on the right or left foot, how his form holds up when he's fatigued, the smallest details that most overlook. If I'm at one of his games, I'm not taking selfies, or walking around the arena shaking hands, or posting pictures to show off my seats or what shoes I'm wearing. I'm in my seat, fixated on every moment. I rarely know who's sitting around me, and if you come up to me during a game, I probably won't even notice you standing there. I'm not being rude. My focus is just elsewhere.

That carries over into every part of my business. You need me to be in this city or country by tonight? I'll make it happen. You need to change our meeting from 11:00 a.m. to 11:00 p.m.? Done. The gym at your hotel is closed? I'll find a new one, or work you out in your room if I have to. I don't stop to think: *That won't work, I had these plans and that appointment and it's too complex and . . .* no. When I'm locked in, that's it. Total focus on our results.

But that's when most people make excuses: *Don't worry about it, things happen. It's a marathon, not a sprint!*

Winning is watching, waiting to see if you're willing to settle for that kind of BS.

I never settle. When a client shows up a half hour late (although the best of the best are never late) and tells me we won't have enough time, I'll tell him: *Oh, really? You got twenty-five minutes? Let's go for twenty-five minutes then. It'll be the most focused twenty-five minutes of your life.*

You didn't have time to finish your work? Yes you did, you just didn't have the focus to finish your work. The time was there. Your head was somewhere else.

Focus is about minutes, not hours or days or years. If I need you for one hour, you can't lose focus at fifty-nine minutes. After that, you can go watch cartoons or call your broker or find your friends. But for that hour, all sixty minutes . . . we sprint.

MJ's focus began the minute he started his workout in the morning, and usually ended when he returned to his hotel or home after a game. For that time, he was centered on what he needed to accomplish in those hours. Nothing was unplanned, and nothing escaped his focus. After that, he could exhale and relax for a short while . . . until the next day when he started all over again. He knew no other way. That was his direct link to Winning. Still is.

Many pro athletes received a lesson in focus during the Covid-19 pandemic, when quarantines and precautions meant playing without fans at the games, and in some cases, living in a secure "bubble" without family or friends. Few could remember the last time they'd played to empty stadiums and arenas: Grade school? The playground? Their entire sporting lives had been filled with parents, friends, family, and eventually, hundreds of thousands of screaming fans. Now, for the first time . . . silence. No one cheering or heckling, no vendors, no tickets to distribute, no worries about where friends or family were sitting. They could hear the sounds of the game; they could hear each other. A completely different experience. Some said it didn't affect their game at all. Some felt that the lack of distraction allowed them to focus more on the game itself, not what was happening on the periphery. Others said that without the crowd buzz, they had a harder time getting into the Zone, where your focus is so heightened you can't even explain it.

Focus isn't the same as the Zone, which we talked about in *Relentless*. The Zone is unconscious; your skills and expertise are so highly developed that you don't have to think about what you're doing, the action just flows. Focus is highly conscious; it requires you to be sharp and aware of every moment, and allows you to work on skills so intently that you eventually no longer have to think about them. You just execute. You can't enter the Zone until you've mastered focus; focus is the training ground.

Think about where you are in your life right now. Maybe you feel you haven't done enough—haven't reached your goals. You're disappointed in yourself because you know you could have done more, but something stopped you. You lost your direction, not for a minute or hour, but for a long, long time.

That's all about lack of focus.

Why do people tend to wait for a loss or disappointment to start focusing? They fail at something, get cut from the team, lose a big sale, don't get the job or the raise—*then* they want to buckle down. *Now* they're going to get serious. Everything is going to change. One question: Why weren't they *already* serious? And how many get hit by that disappointment and *still* don't get focused?

Focus is about controlling your behavior, so it becomes easier to do the right things, and harder to be distracted by the wrong things.

I'm not telling you to stay this way 24/7; you need some distractions that allow you to relax and give your focus a rest—kids, naps, exercise, vacation. Use that time to energize your focus.

But control that time. Choose it. Do it because you want to do it, not because someone demanded it.

Obviously, you can't give everything in your life equal focus and dedication, so whatever you choose to focus on, it better be something you want for yourself, not what someone else wants for you. Because it's impossible to focus with sufficient intensity on something you don't really want.

How do you know if a goal is worth it? Ask yourself three simple questions. And if the answer to all three isn't *yes*, Winning would like you to move on to something else:

- *Do you want to do it?* Is this your idea, or someone else's? Is it your dream, or are you doing it to please others? Because you can't just want it, you have to crave it enough to make it your obsession.

- *Can you do it?* If you're not able, if you don't have the skill or means to make it happen, all the focus in the world isn't going to deliver the results. You must be realistic about what you're capable of achieving, so that you're focusing on something that has at least a chance of working.

- *Is it worth your time?* I mean, really, really worth your time? Will it be worth the sacrifice and commitment and relentless grind? Because Winning wants all of your attention, not just spare moments when you have nothing else to do.

Focus is 100 percent about you. You're not making dinner plans that you don't have time for, you're not running errands that someone else sent you to do, you're not immediately responding to every text and email and call. You're protecting your mental space and creating control for yourself. Those twenty-four hours will still be there waiting for you to choose how to use them. Will you use them to win?

#1.
WINNING IS EVERYTHING

When I started writing this book, I made a list of all the topics I wanted to cover, the things I believe have had the greatest impact on all the winners I've known and watched and experienced.

After I finalized that list—The Winning 13—I had to laugh about the topics that didn't make the cut.

Hard work. Commitment. Teamwork. Leadership. Many others, for sure.

If you got through this whole book, and you're wondering why those things aren't prominently featured, let me assure you, it wasn't an oversight.

I wanted to give you more, because Winning is so much more. Do you really need me to tell you about the importance of hard work and commitment? Like you don't already know that? I didn't want to address the same things everyone else has talked about in thousands of books, over and over. If I'm going to write the book on Winning, I have to write the book no one else has written, because I've seen and learned too much not to share that with you. Most people deliver the expected. That has never worked for my clients, and it has never worked for me.

If you do it like everyone else, you'll *be* like everyone else.

I want you to be so much more.

You already know that Winning requires hard work and commitment. You already know the importance of teamwork and leadership.

Everything you've read in this book is about making those things possible.

You can't achieve those things until you understand—and *use*—what you've read here. You can't put in the hard work until you can control that battlefield in your mind. Your commitment will only be as strong as your resilience. You won't be an effective teammate until you can get your mind stronger than your feelings. You can't be a great leader without understanding how to think for yourself.

People love to talk about a winning attitude, a winning mindset . . . but what does that actually mean? You can't have that attitude or that mindset without actually experiencing what it means to win. You can't learn it from a podcast or read about it in a book—even this one. You can't win by simply absorbing thoughts about Winning. You have to release real energy and perform the action of Winning. It won't grow on its own, it needs your investment and commitment—it needs everything—to grow. You have to take the risk and the action and *feel* it.

You have to experience everything that actually goes into Winning, not just the celebration at the end. If you ever watch a big postgame celebration—I'm talking about a regular season game, not a championship—you'll see that the biggest celebrators usually have the cleanest uniforms.

Sometimes they never even got out of their sweats. Yes, they "won," they're part of the team. But until they've felt it all—everything—they can't know what went into getting there. They just can't.

Remember earlier in this book when we talked about the combination vault you have to crack in order to access Winning? The Winning 13 are the first part of the code.

But there are many other truths that you can absorb and apply—an infinite number, in fact. And it would take many lifetimes to master even a fraction of them.

I told you at the start of this book that each of the 13 is as important as all the others, and that's true. But if I had to pick one that means the most to me, the one that truly sums up what I know about Winning, it's this:

Winning is everything.

Because it is. Every day, in everything you do, your wins are waiting for you. They're everywhere. But they won't wait forever. Stop waiting to be told what you can and can't do. Stop watching others win while you stand on the sidelines wondering when it's going to be your turn. Your turn is now. Long-term goals are great . . . but "long term" isn't promised to anyone. Your skills and opportunities have an expiration date. If you want something, go get it now.

I get so frustrated with those who say they want to win, but show no urgency or drive to actually do it, as if they'll have unlimited years and opportunities to figure it out. As if it's just going to happen eventually. To me, a sense of urgency is the ultimate distinction between those who win and those who watch others win.

That sense of "gotta have it *now*" defined Kobe's spirit.

His impatience was legendary; there was always work to be done and he had zero tolerance for those who wouldn't do it. Every day of his life was about the urgency to win something, anything, everything.

As you've heard me say often in this book, the biggest mistake we make in life is thinking we have time. I frequently talked with Kobe about this. How I wish I'd been wrong.

Remember him when you think you have plenty of time. I think about it every day.

Winners have one fear, and it isn't about losing. They can come back from a loss, they can find another way to win. They fear not having enough time. Not enough days, weeks, months, and years to complete their life's work. Not having everything in place. Not accomplishing everything they dreamed of. Not *finishing*. Most people accept that they won't get to do everything in their lifetime. Winners can't accept that. They need to finish. Everything.

Because ultimately, Winning is immortality. It's your legacy, the culmination of what you've accomplished, what you've built, what you contributed. It's the sum of how you touched those around you, the memories you leave with them, what you've done for others and for yourself. And if you've been successful in your race to greatness, at the end of your life Winning will embrace you, erase your losses, and keep you forever in its Hall of Fame.

Death puts you in Winning's elite club of greatness, where nothing can ever change what you accomplished. Everything you've achieved stays with you. Your race is done.

People say Winning makes them feel alive. And it does. But it also brings you closer to life's end, because the longer it takes to capture your wins, the less time you have to enjoy them, or repeat them, or learn from them. That's the unforgiving race—every day your time grows shorter.

When I was in college I had hanging over my bed a basketball net with a ball in it; it was an award for making a game-winning shot. I used to lay in bed and look at that net, and think about how I learned to play without one; we had a rusty hoop on the broken concrete playground. That was all I ever needed, a ball and a hoop. A net? I thought it was for show. A net slows things down as the ball moves through it, so as a kid I always felt the ball come at me fast and hard.

Ironically, that ball over my bed was never used, never allowed to do what it was meant to do—bounce, roll, fly through the air. Over the years, the net continued to hold it there, immobilized. That's what nets do: trap you, hold you in one place, protect you, sometimes from others, sometimes from yourself.

We all have nets that keep us from doing what we're meant to do.

Don't let that happen to you.

Do everything.

Experience everything. Experiment and wonder and dream and make it all happen. Winners welcome all experiences because they never know which will take them to the next level.

I'm not telling you to "find balance," where you take on a million things that don't help your goals. I'm suggesting you embrace possibility and hope and new ways to learn and think. I'm telling you to dance like nobody's watching, even when they are . . . to let go and let loose, just because you want to. Not for anyone else, but for yourself.

Winners know they're going to lose time, friends, money, courage, and strength—but they never lose belief in themselves, because they're driven to win. They can't accept the alternative.

Most people will encourage you to settle for less. They'll tell you you've done everything you can do, so relax, take it easy, don't take everything so seriously.

Winners wage war against that every day, a relentless campaign against unhappiness, weakness, laziness. What is your daily campaign? How do you repel temptation and doubt? What is your campaign against the urge to just give up? "Let's go!" is not a campaign. "Crushing it" is not a campaign.

Everyone who has finished something has one thing in common: the urge to quit. There's not a winner out there who hasn't thought about quitting at some point. You can't make the commitment to win until you've tasted the urge to quit.

We're all weak sometimes, and we all have the urge to give up. It would be so easy . . . so quiet . . . so calm . . . to just stop the craziness and intensity and pressure and be normal, like everyone else.

Normal, like everyone else.

No thanks.

You may not win at everything. Everyone comes up short in some way. You can't be the strongest person in the world *and* the fastest *and* the smartest *and* the richest. You won't dominate everything. You won't win everything.

But you *will* win. Explore and embrace your weaknesses. Only then can you let go of the fears and inhibitions that hold you back from everything you want. Drive yourself through those boundaries, until you find the thing that excites you and takes you to where you want to go.

Winning is everywhere, like the song that gets stuck in your head that goes around and around and you can't make it stop. Don't stop. Keep going. Every day, keep going.

The pursuit of Winning has defined my life. My desire for it hasn't been about financial gain, or fame, or access to the greatest winners of our time. For me, it has always been about the indescribable rush of satisfaction and pride and sweetness that comes with every win, every time. The high is so high you can only get it from the black market in your head. The darkest place in your mind.

Unfortunately, that rush doesn't last. We make all these down payments in energy, focus, and preparation so we can someday own the luxury of Winning. But Winning can't be owned; we can only rent it, and no matter how much we pay, Winning is still going to change the locks at some point, until we start paying all over again. How can we *not* keep paying? We don't know anything else. We don't *want* to know anything else. Tell us the price. We'll pay it. Please.

My pursuit of Winning has given me so much, yet it

has also cost me much. My health. Relationships. Family. When I felt pain—physically or emotionally—I never backed away from it, I never stepped out of the race I was running. Instead, I conditioned myself to power through it all, sometimes to protect those I love, sometimes to protect myself. I have no problem being a life jacket for others, but have a hard time allowing anyone to save me. I could have changed direction anytime along the way. But it's not who I am. And not for a minute do I regret any of it.

In the final days of my dad's life, he told me the family was now my responsibility. I told him, with the broken heart of a man about to lose his father, that I wasn't as strong as he was.

"You're right," he said. "You're stronger."

I live every day trying to prove him right.

Strength comes in many disguises. Yes, it means being relentless and resilient, and holding up others when you can barely hold up yourself. But there's more to it than showing power and control. It means having the ability to laugh at yourself and see your own flaws. It's the confidence to walk away when it's time, and not look back at what you left behind. It's showing emotion when you feel it, and not faking it when you don't. It's sharing your wins with those who rode along with you, who never left your side and never will.

If you're blessed or fortunate enough to find that person, you've found something as rare as Winning itself.

If you watched *The Last Dance*, you may have seen me become visibly emotional at one point, talking about Michael's commitment to himself, to the fans, to always delivering his best. I never forget what he gave of himself in those years, what he carried on his shoulders and in his heart. It was intense back then, and the memory of it remains intense for me today.

What you didn't see was what came after that.

The director, Jason Hehir, asked me: "Why the emotion?"

I couldn't even speak for a very long moment. And then finally I was able to answer, in words I'd never spoken.

He took a chance on me, I told him. He gave an opportunity to a kid he didn't even know, and allowed me to run with him in his race to greatness, for fifteen years. Aside from my parents, no one has had a greater impact on my life, and I'll never be able to express my gratitude for his belief in me.

We were young men then, and it has been my great pride and pleasure to watch him—and all the great athletes who have trusted me with their careers—grow into the next stage of his life, still looking for things to win. From young men they've grown into fathers and grandfathers; from basketball players they've matured into cultural icons and entrepreneurs and business moguls and broadcasters. I've been blessed beyond description to be in their lives, and to have them in mine.

I love seeing MJ have the freedom to throw his golf clubs into a different automobile every morning, run his businesses, and enjoy his life as a father of five with a beautiful grandbaby. I love seeing Dwyane surrounded by his family, and the pride he takes in his beautiful children, raising them with the freedom to express themselves and be who they really are, without prejudice or judgment. I love watching Charles be Charles on the air, telling it like it is and shaking things up, the same way he played.

I'll never stop wondering what Kobe would have achieved. The world deserved so much more of his brilliance and greatness; he deserved so much more of everything. But I know he and his baby Gianna are together at Winning's head table, laughing at the rest of us, and finding new wins every day.

MJ opened the door for me. I was able to open it for others who gave me their trust, including not just clients but young trainers eager to learn the business.

So when others call me the Godfather, the guru of what I do, I'm humbled and proud. That's Winning to me, the ability to empower others to do what I've done.

I began this book by talking about the hardship and endurance and sacrifice that go into Winning. *Uncivilized. Hard. Nasty. Unpolished. Dirty. Rough. Unforgiving. Unapologetic. Uninhibited.*

That's the reality of racing toward a destination that will do everything possible to make sure you never arrive. It's tough and unforgiving, and it's supposed to be.

But at the end, and even along the way, there is joy.

There must always be joy.

No matter how intense and competitive and driven you may be, don't shut out the opportunity to be in the moment, to embrace what you have, and hold on to it for as long as you can. Take time in your life for true fun and happiness and joy and laughter, wherever you can find it. It doesn't make you weak to enjoy your life and appreciate the things that give you satisfaction and a sense of accomplishment.

For me, those things aren't necessarily the championships or rings. Some of my greatest achievements have involved seeing the joy in my client's eyes after performing at an entirely new level. Knowing I made my parents proud. Speaking to an audience and seeing them "get it." Working with my Down & Dirty mentoring groups and hearing about their wins, over and over. Remaining authentic and true to who I am. Staying true to those I love and who love me unconditionally. And above all, being a dad.

Whatever you dream for yourself, whatever you're chasing, stay with it. Believe in it. Fight for it like your life depends on it, because it does.

Winning is watching. It's waiting for you at the finish line, with a message:

Welcome.

The race is over.

The price has been paid.

For now.

YOUR NEXT WIN IS WAITING

These pages are for you to fill with your wins . . . past, present, and future.

Wins are everywhere. Recognize them, enjoy them for a moment, and build on them. Plan for what's next. Write them down. Winning is waiting.

_____

_____

_____

_____

_____

_____

_____

_____

_____

_____

_____

_____

_____

_____

_____

_____

_____

_____

_____

_____

_____

_____

_____

ACKNOWLEDGMENTS

I was given a pen to put my thoughts, education, and experiences into this book about Winning. I had the option of writing something beautiful, or meaningful, or even hurtful. Either way, the opportunity to write this book was a gift, and I had to decide how to use that gift. My deepest gratitude to my co-writer and agent, Shari Wenk, for working with me to pass this gift along to you, wrapping it and giving the opportunity to so many to unwrap the gift of *Winning*.

Winning is about having the right allies. I am grateful for my partnership with Scribner, especially executive editor Rick Horgan, who understood that Winning isn't always about the celebration but the unseen work and unrelenting obstacles that get in the way of success. I was fortunate to work with the entire Scribner team on *Relentless* as well; thank you for believing in me.

To the thousands of athletes who allowed me to be part of their wins, you'll never know how much I cherish and appreciate our journey together.

And to the many, many readers who read *Relentless* and shared their stories and experiences with me . . . let's win.

ABOUT THE AUTHOR

Tim S. Grover is the CEO of Attack Athletics, Inc., which he founded in 1989. World-renowned for his work with Michael Jordan, Kobe Bryant, Dwyane Wade, Charles Barkley, and thousands of athletes and business professionals, he appears around the world as a keynote speaker and consultant to business leaders, athletes, and elite achievers in every field, teaching the principles of relentless drive, results-driven performance, and mental toughness.

Tim is the author of the national bestseller *Relentless: From Good to Great to Unstoppable* and *Winning: The Unforgiving Race to Greatness*, and creator of the digital training platform The Relentless System.

He earned his bachelor's degree in kinesiology and his master's degree in exercise science at the University of Illinois–Chicago. A former NCAA Division I basketball player at the school, he received its Lifetime Achievement Award in 2010 and at that time was inducted into the UIC Hall of Fame. He is based in Chicago.

For more about Tim Grover, please visit www.TimGrover.com.